Helping Homeschoolers in the Library

Adrienne Furness

AMERICAN LIBRARY ASSOCIATION
Chicago 2008

While extensive effort has gone into ensuring the reliability of information appearing in this book, the publisher makes no warranty, express or implied, on the accuracy or reliability of the information, and does not assume and hereby disclaims any liability to any person for any loss or damage caused by errors or omissions in this publication.

Printed on 50-pound white offset, a pH-neutral stock, and bound in 10-point cover stock by Victor Graphics.

The paper used in this publication meets the minimum requirements of American National Standard for Information Sciences—Permanence of Paper for Printed Library Materials, ANSI Z39.48-1992. ∞

Library of Congress Cataloging-in-Publication Data
Furness, Adrienne.
   Helping homeschoolers in the library / Adrienne Furness.
      p. cm.
   Includes bibliographical references and index.
   ISBN-13: 978-0-8389-0955-3 (alk. paper)
   ISBN-10: 0-8389-0955-8 (alk. paper)
   1. Libraries and home schooling. 2. Home schooling—United States. I. Title.
Z718.75.F87 2008
027.6—dc22   2007036287

Copyright © 2008 by the American Library Association. All rights reserved except those which may be granted by Sections 107 and 108 of the Copyright Revision Act of 1976.

ISBN-13: 978-0-8389-0955-3
ISBN-10: 0-8389-0955-8

Printed in the United States of America

12 11 10 09 08   5 4 3 2 1

CONTENTS

PREFACE   v

ACKNOWLEDGMENTS   vii

PART I
DEFINING HOMESCHOOLERS

1. The Truth about Homeschooling   1
2. The Unschooling Movement   11
3. Homeschooling for Religious Reasons: Conservative Protestants   20
4. Homeschooling for Religious Reasons: Other Religions   26
5. Homeschooling Youth with Special Needs   33
6. Other Homeschooling Groups and Trends   42

PART II
SERVING HOMESCHOOLERS

7. Connecting with Homeschoolers in Your Community   55
8. Creating Programs with Homeschoolers in Mind   70
9. Building a Special Collection   82
10. Helping Homeschoolers in the Library: It's Easier Than You Think   93

APPENDIX

"Serving Homeschoolers" Grant Application: New York State
Library Parent and Child Library Services, 2005–2007   99

GLOSSARY   115

BIBLIOGRAPHY   119

INDEX   133

PREFACE

According to a study by the National Center for Education Statistics, *Homeschooling in the United States: 2003*, there were more than a million children being homeschooled in 2003. This report also revealed that 78 percent of homeschooling parents used the public library as a source of learning materials, more than any other source—even edging out catalogs and publishers that market specifically to homeschoolers. This quantifies something we already know: homeschooling is a rising trend, and it's one that has a tremendous impact on public libraries. Most librarians are well aware of homeschoolers in their communities because they are among the most frequent and heaviest borrowers, but many librarians struggle to find ways to serve this population. In the face of evidence to the contrary, inaccurate and often negative stereotypes persist of homeschoolers as either religious zealots or neo-hippies. Many librarians are reluctant to approach homeschoolers in their community or engage them in conversation simply because they don't understand what homeschooling is all about.

This book seeks to break stereotypes and educate librarians about some of the major reasons parents choose to homeschool their children. It also gives librarians the information and tools they need to develop policies, programs, and services that support homeschoolers in their communities. The first half of the book explores philosophies and trends in homeschooling and places them in context, giving librarians enough knowledge to begin to understand homeschoolers' wide variety of needs along with resources and a vocabulary that will allow them to approach homeschoolers with some confidence. The second half of the book deals specifically with building library programs and services for the homeschooling population.

Helping Homeschoolers in the Library is designed to work well both for those who wish to read straight through and those who prefer to jump in and out of particular sections as the mood strikes. Throughout, it includes profiles of homeschoolers, writers, thinkers, librarians, and others who are active in some way in the homeschooling movement. It is my hope that these profiles add the same depth to the content being covered for my readers as they did for me while I was talking to these amazingly diverse, intelligent, committed, and inspiring people.

This work is meant to be a starting point and is by no means a comprehensive history or explication of every facet of the homeschooling world. The nature of homeschooling is that it evolves as children and families evolve. Websites, periodicals, and organizations come and go. Laws and regulations are changing all the time. Throughout the book, I provide resources for further information for readers who wish to explore and learn more. Readers would do well to seek out resources mentioned in the context of chapters, in the notes, and in the bibliography, which provides a core homeschooling collection list as well as important homeschooling periodicals. I also provide updates from my continued exploration of the homeschooling world on my Homeschooling and Libraries blog at http://homeschoolingandlibraries.wordpress.com.

The good news is that public libraries and homeschoolers share many values. In children's departments, we support and encourage parents' roles as their children's first teachers. We empower parents to screen their children's borrowing. We work with children to help them explore their interests and passions and to build a solid foundation for lifelong learning. Like homeschooling pioneer John Holt, librarians believe that learning isn't something that only happens in a certain place during certain hours on a schoolday. We believe that people's quests to reach their full potential take many directions and forms, and we believe in the importance of the life of the mind. Homeschoolers embrace these aspects of public libraries' traditional mission and take them a step further. They believe so strongly in their roles as their children's first teachers that they choose to hold on to that role instead of handing it over to institutions. Regardless of their philosophical leanings, like librarians, homeschoolers recognize the importance of learning and the impact learning will have on the rest of their children's lives.

The even better news is that most of the programs and services libraries develop with homeschoolers in mind also serve their communities as a whole. As is the case with so many special populations, making an effort and opening the lines of communication are key. This book introduces you to a lot of people, philosophies, and trends, but it is my sincerest hope that you walk away wanting to learn more. Talk to the homeschoolers in your service area. Try attending conferences, meetings, and curriculum fairs. These events can be intimidating at first, especially when participants have strong beliefs you don't share, but they may also surprise you. Homeschoolers remind me again and again of how much there is to learn in this world, and that is a beautiful thing.

ACKNOWLEDGMENTS

When I started writing this book, I had no idea that the endeavor would make me so acutely aware of how much I rely on the wonderful people who surround me. First thanks must go to Kim Bolan for passing my name along, and second thanks to ALA Editions for liking my idea and making this process one of the most rewarding of my career.

For the past few years, rock star librarians Cathy Henderson, Cathy Kyle, Jennifer Lindsey, and Melissa Painton have worked with me in an effort to better serve homeschoolers in Monroe County through a New York State Library Parent and Child Services Grant. I learned and gained more than I can say through their friendship, dedication, and hard work, and I don't think this book would exist without them. I would also like to thank the dozens of homeschooling families who have taught me so much through the years, particularly over the past year and a half and particularly those who have opened up their lives to all as subjects of profiles throughout this book.

My friends and coworkers at the Webster Public Library are a continual source of support and inspiration. I want to particularly thank Terri Bennett for unfailing encouragement, Lisa Wemett for good advice, Olivia Durant for new words, Diane Kozlowski for diversion, Penny Deisinger for organization, Greg Benoit for the promise of help with publicity, Marcia and the rest of the Weinerts for four hundred million things I can't possibly list, Jewyl Bierma for dedication, Sarah Hodges for enthusiasm, and Xandi DiMatteo and Elizabeth Kwiatkowski for research assistance.

Jeffrey Yoshi Lee took my publicity photos, Chuck and Kelly Scroger were available to debate the minutiae of English construction, and Craig Gable always acknowledges me. Tracy Cretelle and Heidi Lux read multiple drafts and helped me every time I started to panic. I don't know what I would have done without Jason Poole. My blog friends at watat.com have made every day a little more interesting. The staff of the Leaf and Bean continues to provide me with my daily dose of community and caffeine, which makes me just a little smarter.

Finally, I thank my mom and dad, Michele Iselo and Patrick Pettinelli, for all the times they didn't say no. This book wouldn't be complete without Jennifer Behrens. Tammy, Ron, Lucas, and Max Pritchard love me so much more than I deserve. I dedicate this book to Tammy, in the hope of many more years in which to continue homeschooling ourselves.

PART I
DEFINING HOMESCHOOLERS

1

The Truth about Homeschooling

Like librarians, homeschoolers are plagued by stereotypes. People tend to think of homeschooling as a fringe movement perpetuated by new-age hippies or fundamentalist Protestants. They worry that homeschooled children are too sheltered, that they aren't being socialized, and that they aren't learning enough.

Although it is true that homeschooling has grown out of the left-wing alternative schools movement of the 1960s and '70s and flourished among conservative Christians in the past two decades, homeschoolers have never been easy to categorize, and the movement is now too large to dismiss. The National Center for Education Statistics estimates that there were approximately 1.1 million students being homeschooled in 2003, a 29 percent increase over their 1999 estimate.[1] Articles about homeschooling have appeared in recent issues of *Business Week, Ebony, Ladies Home Journal, Good Housekeeping, People Weekly,* and *Family Circle*. As the population continues to grow, homeschooling is becoming part of the mainstream and comprises a variety of people who cannot be captured in a snapshot.

A BRIEF HISTORY OF HOMESCHOOLING

Most homeschoolers are quick to point out that state-controlled compulsory education is a relatively new phenomenon in the United States, and they often list such influential American thinkers as George Washington,

Thomas Jefferson, and Abraham Lincoln among the ranks of successful homeschoolers. A closer examination shows that these luminaries were more commonly educated through a combination of homeschooling and institutional schooling, but the fact remains that they lived at a time when most children were educated at home and academics took an unquestioned back seat to household chores, particularly the demands of farm life. States began to enact compulsory schooling laws only in the second half of the nineteenth century, and many states didn't adopt them until well into the twentieth century.

Of course, as long as there have been compulsory schooling laws, there have been people who have opted out of public schools. Catholics built their parochial school system as an alternative to schools that promoted Protestant religions, and there have always been families who have had enough of a problem with government-controlled schools that they chose—through much of the twentieth century, illegally—to keep their children at home. Even so, people didn't start talking about homeschooling as a serious option until the early 1960s when educational theorist John Holt began advocating a child-centered and child-led approach to education in his books *How Children Fail* and *How Children Learn*. As we explore in further detail in chapter 2, Holt ultimately decided that institutional schools were never going to be the best way to educate children, and he began encouraging parents to "unschool" children at home. The unschooling movement grew over the next two decades, but the homeschooling population truly began to explode in the late 1980s and early '90s as homeschooling gained hold in the conservative Protestant world we explore in chapter 3. Through the '90s and into the new millennium, homeschooling has become normalized to the point that it is being embraced by people from a surprising number of backgrounds. This growth has spawned a wealth of publications, products, and services aimed specifically at homeschoolers.

LEGAL ISSUES

Homeschooling became officially legal in all fifty states only in the early 1990s, so many pioneers in the homeschooling movement kept their children home under the threat of legal action. Today, laws pertaining to homeschoolers vary widely from state to state, and there are still some homeschoolers who choose to disregard state legal requirements. It is important for librarians to understand that many homeschoolers rightly

> ### RESOURCES
>
> ## Websites
>
> About.com Homeschooling: http://homeschooling.about.com
> > This site's pop-up and other ads are irritating, but the site provides a great deal of information and a wealth of links to topics of interest to homeschoolers and the librarians who seek to serve them. This is a good way to find some hard-to-find resources on some of the lower-profile niches in the homeschooling world.
>
> Homeschool Diner: http://www.homeschooldiner.com
> > Homeschooling mom Julie Shepherd Knapp maintains this site devoted to homeschooling in all its forms. The site has information particularly useful to those new to homeschooling, including a "Click-o-matic Homeschool Quiz" as well as useful, concise summaries of a variety homeschooling approaches and philosophies. Knapp includes annotated links to learning resources organized by topic and also maintains an associated discussion list on Yahoo Groups. This is the most professional and useful site geared toward all homeschoolers rather than one particular group.
>
> National Home Education Research Institute (NHERI): http://www.nheri.org
> > Founded in 1990 by researcher and homeschooling advocate Brian D. Ray, this nonprofit organization devoted to research disseminates information pertaining to homeschooling. Ray encounters many of the research issues that plague the field (such as the difficulty of obtaining sizable and representative samples), but few people have studied homeschooling as devotedly as Ray, and his work is worth critical examination.

view the public library as an institution connected to the same government that runs the school systems they've rejected and whose scrutiny, even if they are following applicable laws, they wish to avoid. You need only talk to one homeschooler who has been visited by a representative of a social services department to understand why.

Finding out what laws apply to homeschoolers in your state is usually a simple matter of consulting state statutes. State department of education websites as well as state and local homeschool support groups can also be good sources of legal information. Support groups often go a step further to provide practical information about how families can interpret and comply with state laws. Local school districts are generally not experts in homeschooling and are notorious for giving out incorrect and misleading information, and it is vitally important that parents know exactly what the law requires. Laws in some states are fairly lax. Texas, for example, currently doesn't require parents to fill out any paperwork or do any reporting. Other states have more stringent requirements. In homeschooling circles, Pennsylvania is often cited as a "difficult" state because its laws require parents to file a notarized affidavit with the school district, maintain a portfolio for each student, and have each child take regular standardized tests.

Homeschooling laws are also being challenged with some frequency, both by people who would like to see homeschoolers regulated more and those who would like to see them regulated less. The Home School Legal Defense Association, a conservative Protestant group, maintains information about laws in each state, laws under consideration in each state, as well as any court cases they are involved in on their website (www.hslda.org). It's worth noting, as we see in chapter 3, that not all homeschoolers support this association's perspective or agenda.

THE HOMESCHOOLING FAMILY

According to the best available research, homeschooled children are most likely to come from larger two-parent families in which one parent, most often the mother, is home full-time. Additionally, homeschoolers are more likely than their institutionally schooled peers to live in urban areas and have parents whose educational attainment is a bachelor's degree or higher.[2] None of these statistics are particularly surprising. Some single-parent families and families in which both parents work full-time manage to homeschool, but these lifestyles present obvious challenges. Urban areas have more community-based educational opportunities as well as larger populations with which to network and find support. And parents who have pursued advanced degrees might be more willing to make the investment in their children's education that homeschooling requires.

To be sure, school is one of the United States' most basic institutions, and most families don't reject it lightly. Although stereotypes have evolved from John Holt's unschooling philosophy and the homeschooling trend among conservative Protestants, most parents have multiple reasons for keeping their children out of institutional schools. Of parents surveyed by the National Center for Education Statistics, 85 percent reported that they homeschool because they have concerns about the environment and safety of institutional schools. Other reasons include concerns about religious and moral instruction, dissatisfaction with the quality of academic instruction, and the fact that their children have unique educational, physical, or mental health needs.[3] In a recent conversation, *Practical Homeschooling* magazine publisher Mary Pride pointed out that once there was a more uniform homeschooling culture, but today that isn't the case: "Librarians would do well to remember that the homeschooler they see today could be a public schooler or private schooler tomorrow . . . and the public or private schooler they see today could be a homeschooler tomorrow." Some homeschoolers are strong homeschooling advocates, whereas others are homeschooling in response to specific circumstances and don't have an issue with public schools per se. Some families just aren't sure.

Those unfamiliar with homeschooling often have questions about how homeschooling families schedule their time. Families tend to fall somewhere within a range from extremely structured to extremely unstructured, although most live happily somewhere in the middle. The majority of homeschoolers follow an academic year that more or less mirrors that of institutional schools. This can be a matter of practicality in states that require homeschooling families to observe a certain number of schooldays or amount of "seat time," and some families just like the traditional academic calendar. That said, many choose to homeschool year-round, and most homeschoolers readily adjust their schedules to accommodate travel or special projects. Some families opt for a partial schedule on typical vacations or holidays, focusing either on particular interests or areas where children are struggling. Since homeschooling becomes an integral part of a family's daily home life, very few homeschoolers take the kind of total break from schooling most Americans associate with the summer or spring break.

Daily homeschooling schedules are even more varied. Most homeschoolers who use structured curriculum packages, correspondence courses, workbooks, and the like do their formal, sit-down coursework in the morning. Some families go so far as to take the phone off the hook for several hours every morning to make sure they aren't interrupted. Some families do a little bit of each subject every day, whereas others select different subjects each day; Monday and Wednesday might be reserved for math and science, for instance, Tuesday and Thursday for language arts and social studies, and Friday for field trips. Most homeschoolers have outside commitments such as volunteering, paying jobs, support group meetings, classes, and community events that contribute to their homeschooling plan and also impact their daily and weekly schedules. Many homeschoolers try to keep outside commitments to the afternoon, but that is by no means universal or even a majority. A Catholic family, for example, may choose to attend morning mass every Wednesday; a family with a child interested in working with children may find a morning volunteer placement that allows their child to work with preschoolers. To get more of an idea of what all this looks like in practice, take some time to peruse the profiles of homeschoolers and homeschooling families included throughout this book.

Another big issue families have to contend with is the dizzying array of curriculum packages, study programs, correspondence schools, and other educational products designed specifically for homeschoolers. Settling on a homeschooling approach and selecting curriculums can be overwhelming, especially to new homeschoolers. Most families do a great deal of research and make their own decisions, but they can also hire one of the fee-based consultants who specialize in navigating homeschooling options and designing individualized programs for students. Families acquire learning materials via the Internet, mail-order companies, traditional educational publishers, teacher supply stores, and Christian bookstores. More and more mainstream bookstores are devoting shelf space to homeschooling materials, and some areas have enough homeschoolers to support brick-and-mortar stores entirely devoted to homeschooling. Even with all these retail options, study after study confirms that homeschoolers rely heavily on public libraries as a primary or supplemental source of learning materials, and homeschoolers are often among any library's heaviest borrowers.

THE HOMESCHOOLED CHILD

People who ask questions about homeschooling are most concerned about the welfare of homeschooled children. Do they learn enough? Do they become responsible citizens? Are they able to function when they leave their homes? We see homeschoolers making headlines in such high-profile events as the National Geographic Bee, the Scripps Howard National Spelling Bee, and even the Miss America Pageant—but are these children the exception or the rule? Researchers have been grappling with these questions for decades in their often frustrated attempts to wrest statistically significant data from a small and extremely diverse population that is perhaps best united in its tendency to prefer privacy. Still, research has revealed some useful data and trends.

Although numerous studies have examined homeschoolers' academic achievement, no researcher has been able to prove that homeschooled children are faring substantially better or worse than their institutionally schooled peers. Studies generally indicate that homeschoolers either do as well as or better than other students in various measures of achievement, although some studies have suggested that homeschooled children are more verbal and less mathematically inclined. In most of these studies, though, the differences are too small to be truly significant, and there aren't enough reliable studies to draw solid conclusions.

Perhaps the greater indication of homeschoolers' academic success is the number of colleges that are now accepting and even recruiting homeschooled students, so much so that the *Journal of College Admission* devoted its entire fall 2004 issue to the subject of homeschooling and homeschoolers. Even extremely competitive and conservative Ivy League schools are accepting and sometimes offering scholarships to homeschoolers.

The other main concern people have about homeschoolers has to do with their socialization. Many homeschooling advocates point out that no one has yet proved that institutional schools provide healthy socialization experiences, and they go further to argue that the multigenerational environment most homeschooled children live in more correctly mirrors the world of adults. Aside from the fact that homeschoolers tend to come from larger families, they participate in church groups, scouting, homeschooling groups, 4-H clubs, organized sports, and lessons of all types. Most homeschooling support groups offer meetings, special classes, and even field trips. Far from being socially isolated, research bears out that most homeschooling families are active and involved in their communities.

THE FUTURE OF HOMESCHOOLING

Homeschoolers can be an opinionated bunch, and there are always debates raging within the homeschooling community. Mitchell L. Stevens's fascinating book-length study of the homeschooling movement, *Kingdom of Children*, explores the division between those who would see more structure in homeschooling and those who would see less, a division that is just as important now as when the book was published in 2001. Today there is increasing interest and debate over exactly what constitutes home

PROFILE

Austin Webb

When people hear about a homeschooled teen scoring 1600 on the SAT exam and courting offers from several universities, they might picture a prodigy who was reading as a toddler, doing long division in kindergarten, and spending most of his time as a child and teen studying. Austin Webb's homeschooling journey began when his parents decided to pull him out of school after first grade in the midst of school consolidations and in response to his difficulties learning how to read. As Webb puts it, "To some extent the decision to homeschool was heavily influenced by logistics. However, I think my parents also knew that they could do a better job and that I would need special attention to reach my goals in later years." Webb describes himself as a "somewhat" late reader, and he hated working on math until he picked up a geometry textbook at the age of fifteen, when suddenly, he says, "everything clicked."

After earning a perfect SAT score a few years later, Webb had offers from such prestigious universities as MIT, Harvard, and Duke, but he ultimately accepted a scholarship to begin his studies in mathematics at the California Institute of Technology, with the ultimate goal of studying theoretical physics. Far from being a stereotypical science nerd, Webb has a well-rounded slate of interests, including a love of history and a talent for writing. In addition to his studies, he's written articles for *Practical Homeschooling* magazine about how homeschoolers can best prepare for college. According to Webb, one of the advantages of homeschooling is a less scheduled life that allows families and individuals to take advantage of opportunities as they arise. His opportunities included travel, an Eagle Scout project, and the ability to devote himself to mathematics when the time was right. As Austin Webb says, "The whole point of homeschooling, in my mind at least, is that you can't generalize what works for a particular kid, or a particular family."

schooling. Take, for instance, the Edmonds Homeschool Resource Center (http://school.Edmonds.wednet.edu/ehrc/) in Edmonds, Washington. This "alternative" school is legally considered a public school in the Edmonds School District. It has a faculty, employs support staff, and offers several organized classes. It has a library, a computer lab, and a career center. Families register with the school and are held to certain requirements. Some homeschoolers would say that families operating in this environment are not really homeschooling; others (David Guterson, author of *Family Matters: Why Homeschooling Makes Sense*, for one) would argue that this is a valuable support system more districts should provide.

Similarly, California has a large number of "home charter schools" serving thousands of students. On the books, these children are enrolled in a public charter school, but they do all their work at home. They are, in effect, no more or less homeschooled than children whose parents homeschool based on a packaged curriculum or, even further complicating matters, children enrolled in correspondence schools or one of the increasingly popular Internet-based schools. Homeschoolers say that there are as many different ways to homeschool as there are homeschoolers, and, as homeschooling and technology continue to grow, that will become more and more true.

HOMESCHOOLERS AND LIBRARIES

The Pareto principle tells us that 20 percent of the people who walk through the doors of our libraries generate 80 percent of our business. Homeschoolers are part of that vital 20 percent in most communities. Not all homeschoolers are library users, but homeschoolers who do use the library tend to be heavy users. It is not unusual to hear of homeschooling families—even individuals—with more than one hundred items checked out on their cards at one time.

Homeschoolers have clear and obvious information needs. Most packaged curriculums require or suggest outside reading, and even the most curriculum-driven families tend to encourage children to explore subjects of particular interest through books, videos, and other media. Unschoolers and families who design their own curriculums have even greater needs. Most homeschooling families operate on relatively modest incomes, so the library can help them stretch dollars while also stretching their imaginations and interests.

Although most homeschoolers are frequent users and strong library supporters, some don't use the library as often as they might—or at all. Some homeschoolers report feeling disliked or misunderstood by library staff, and some library practices—item limits, short borrowing periods, heavy overdue fines, and user fees—can become barriers to service. Sometimes one hears a nightmare story about a library staff member calling a truant officer or telling a homeschooler that she doesn't think homeschooling is a good idea, but that's a rarity. Ultimately, some homeschoolers won't trust a government-funded institution no matter what the staff does.

Librarians who wish to gain support in the homeschooling community would do well to start developing relationships with the homeschoolers who use their libraries; learn who some of your homeschoolers are, talk to them, find out what kind of homeschoolers they are, let them know what resources are available. A small investment of time and energy can foster connections, gratitude, and increased library use. Information spreads by word of mouth among homeschoolers, and homeschoolers are only too happy to spread the word about excellent resources.

NOTES

1. Daniel Princiotta and Stacey Bielick, *Homeschooling in the United States: 2003* (Washington, DC: National Center for Education Statistics, 2005), iii. Available online at http://nces.ed.gov/pubs2006/homeschool/.
2. Ibid., 9–10.
3. Ibid., 13.

2

The Unschooling Movement

Homeschooling and *unschooling* are not synonyms. When John Holt first began using the word *unschooling*, he was referring to the process of taking children out of school. But the term has evolved to describe a particular homeschooling philosophy, one that encourages child-led learning in real-world situations rather than adherence to a curriculum and the types of teaching methods typically used in schools. Unschooling is at the core of homeschooling. Although only a minority of homeschoolers today would describe themselves as *officially* unschooling, unschoolers are the pioneers of the homeschooling movement and almost all homeschooling families incorporate some elements of unschooling into their daily routines, whether they call it unschooling or not.

As a philosophy and a movement, unschooling began in the early 1960s with the writings of educational theorist John Holt. Published in 1964, Holt's first book, *How Children Fail*, documents the ways children avoid their work, respond to pressure, and don't learn what we think and hope they're learning in the classroom. Hot on its heels, his second book, *How Children Learn*, examines the ways preschoolers so effectively go about exploring their world. In it, Holt begins to wonder how adults might be able to support and encourage this type of learning to continue through the elementary school years and into adulthood.

GROWING WITHOUT SCHOOLING AND HOLT ASSOCIATES

When Holt first began writing, he was looking for ways to reform schools and classrooms to make them more effective, a task that proved more difficult than he imagined as he encountered countless teachers and administrators who were more interested in preserving the status quo than in what children were actually learning. He worked a variety of teaching jobs while he was writing and after he published his first books, but he finally settled into a career as a full-time author and lecturer and formed his consulting firm, Holt Associates (www.holtgws.com), in 1969. It wasn't until the mid-'70s that Holt decided that the idea of having a designated place for learning was misguided and first began to talk about and advocate homeschooling.

In 1977, Holt began the influential newsletter *Growing without Schooling* (GWS) as a forum and source of support for families who were looking for learning opportunities outside the traditional school framework and had pulled their children out of school entirely. It is important to remember that Holt began publishing GWS in an environment that was relatively hostile to the idea of homeschooling. Even more than today, homeschooling in the late '70s was seen as an aberration, and the practice was considered flatly illegal in most states. GWS ceased publication in 2001 after twenty-four years and 143 issues, many of which are still available for purchase through FUN Books of Pasadena, Maryland (www.funbooks.com). GWS wasn't just important to the unschooling movement; it was a key element in the formation of the larger homeschooling movement and helped pave the way for the infinite variety of homeschoolers we see today.

HOW UNSCHOOLING WORKS

Holt's ideas evolved throughout his life and numerous writings, but essentially his beliefs revolve around the idea that children don't do much meaningful learning in school—partly because school is cut off from the real world and partly because children are being asked to spend most of their time doing things that don't interest them. If left to their own devices, Holt theorized, children would continue to learn as they do as preschoolers—boldly experimenting, asking questions, and displaying a great deal of ingenuity and interest in the world. Holt believed that subjects don't need to be learned in a particular sequence, and he also believed in the benefits of repetition and failure. He pointed out that many real-world tasks—cooking, cleaning, carpentry, budgeting, and the like—would lead children to want to learn about subjects such as math, science, reading, and writing, and he thought that the serious study of almost any subject would lead to knowledge in other areas. To the uninitiated, Holt's ideas sound radical and alarming, but the evidence suggests that unschooled children do just fine.

Of course, unschooling families operate on a spectrum. For some, unschooling is very much a philosophical decision. For others, it is something they come to through the process of trying to figure out what works best for their circumstances. Some go so far as to reject formal lessons and organized activities of all types, but those families are rare. Some families won't allow a textbook, workbook, or worksheet to cross their thresholds; others utilize these tools as needed. Unschooling parents often talk about being resources and guides for their children. They are on hand to answer questions, explore topics, and point their children to solid resources. Because of this, unschoolers can be among any public library's most devoted homeschooling patrons, visiting the library frequently and checking out a lot of materials.

Most unschoolers don't follow a rigid schedule, and they certainly don't set aside particular times to do schoolwork. They don't think of themselves as doing schoolwork at all; they think of themselves as living life and learning together. Some unschoolers can be critical of other types of homeschoolers who they feel re-create school in their homes, something of which no unschooler would want to be accused; similarly, other homeschoolers can be critical of unschoolers, who they see as undisciplined and lax in their duty to their children. Unschoolers make a conscious effort not to get caught up in typical developmental timetables. If an unschooled child doesn't want to learn how to read until he's a little older, unschooling parents do their best to accept that and trust that the child will get to it eventually.

PHONICS VERSUS WHOLE LANGUAGE

It would be hard to find anyone who wouldn't agree that one of the most important goals of education is to learn how to read, and unschoolers are no exception. A majority of professional educators have come to realize that reading is most successfully taught through a combination of phonics and whole-language methods, but the debate about phonics and whole-language approaches to reading rages on in the homeschooling community just as it has in its institutional counterpart. Unschoolers tend to be on the whole-language side of things and believe wholeheartedly in the importance of reading to children daily and maintaining a large library of high-quality books in their homes. That said, many unschoolers support the growth of reading skills through teaching phonics in any number of formal or informal ways. One thing true unschoolers won't do is to attempt to teach their children phonics or any other way to read before their children show an interest in learning how to read.

UNSCHOOLING RESOURCES

Unschoolers often talk of seeing the world as their classroom. In practical terms, this means unschoolers tend to prefer learning with things that one might have around the house anyway: hammers, measuring cups, magnets, shovels, plants, animals. Unschooling parents believe in giving their children ready access to a wide variety of materials. One often hears unschoolers talk about leaving something around the house in the hope (often rewarded) that a child will pick it up and start exploring it.

Even with all their talk of using real-world items, unschoolers, like other homeschoolers, tend to believe in high-quality educational materials like books, blocks, Legos, and other manipulatives. Many unschoolers use Cuisenaire rods, for example, which children can play with, but the rods can also aid in the understanding of a wide variety of mathematical concepts. A faction of unschoolers believes in providing children with high-quality, professional-grade art materials that an adult artist might use, but almost all unschoolers have a healthy supply of art materials on hand. Many families have binoculars, magnifying glasses, prisms, microscopes, telescopes, and other pieces of scientific equipment. Musical instruments and recorded music are also common sights in unschooling homes. All of these materials can be found in many homeschooling environments, but whereas in some homeschooling families these objects might be part of a more formal lesson, unschooling families seek to use these materials to further the exploration of their interests as part of their ongoing business of living.

RESOURCES

Selected Electronic Discussion Lists

LivingMathForum: http://groups.yahoo.com/group/LivingMathForum/
> An "on-topic" electronic discussion list dedicated to incorporating learning about math into daily life in a holistic way.

Radical Unschoolers List: http://groups.yahoo.com/group/RUL/
> A busy electronic discussion list open to all families.

Unschooling Canada: http://groups.yahoo.com/group/Unschooling_Canada/
> An electronic discussion list for Canadian unschoolers.

Unschooling Teens: http://groups.yahoo.com/group/unschooling_teens/
> An electronic discussion list dedicated to unschooling children ages eleven and up.

UnschoolingDiscussion: http://groups.google.com/group/UnschoolingDiscussion/
> A general electronic discussion list devoted to unschooling.

Unskoolbkshop: http://groups.yahoo.com/group/unskoolbkshop/
> An electronic discussion list that facilitates swapping materials related to unschooling.

TESTING, DIPLOMAS, AND OTHER FORMALITIES

Even more than with other forms of homeschooling, people new to unschooling question how children raised without tests, curriculums, and other standard measurements of achievement get into college and make their way in the world. Unschoolers don't agree with each other on many issues, but one thing that unites them is their dislike of testing, especially the dreaded standardized test. Some states derail unschoolers' attempts to keep their children's lives test free by requiring them to take regular exams. In states that don't require testing, most unschoolers don't face difficult decisions until they begin to consider college and whether to take the SAT or an equivalent exam. Some opt to take the tests; others find a variety of creative ways to avoid them. For example, many unschooled children take their first steps toward college at fifteen or sixteen when they enroll in community college courses in subjects of particular interest. Colleges open to homeschoolers, which are increasingly common, sometimes accept these courses as proof of a candidate's ability to handle college-level work and waive standardized test requirements.

Transcripts and diplomas are another concern. Families who follow standard curriculums have an easier time creating their own transcripts, but many an unschooler manages it as well. Group activities such as scouting, sports, camps, and private lessons can give an unschooling transcript a little more structure and the look of something colleges are used to seeing. Some unschoolers put together portfolios as an alternative or supplement to a transcript.

Diplomas are another sticky wicket. Most states don't allow homeschoolers of any kind to earn a regular state diploma. Some homeschoolers obtain a GED or a diploma issued by their parents, a homeschooling organization, or a correspondence program. This is not the path most unschoolers take; most of them don't acknowledge the validity of an institutional education and its tools, and so to them a diploma is meaningless. Some unschoolers who are particularly concerned about official documentation enroll in a correspondence program such as the Clonlara School's (www.clonlara.org) Home Based Education Program, which is unschooler friendly and allows students to build an official transcript and earn a diploma in a program they essentially design themselves.

Even though unschoolers have deliberately chosen a nontraditional path, they share the same concerns other parents have about their children's opportunities to pursue whatever careers they choose. Books such as Cafi Cohen's *Homeschoolers' College Admissions Handbook: Preparing 12- to 18-Year-Olds for Success in the College of Their Choice* and *And What about College? How Homeschooling Leads to Admissions to the Best Colleges and Universities* provide guidance and reassurance of particular interest to unschooling families facing these issues.

UNSCHOOLING AUTHORS

Holt is not the only author to offer insights into unschooling. Unschooling families are also guided by the work of other authors from a variety of disciplines. Many point to the influence of Alfie Kohn's *Punished by Rewards:*

The Trouble with Gold Stars, Incentive Plans, A's, Praise, and Other Bribes, a treatise on the long-term futility of extrinsic motivation and how to build and support intrinsic motivation in children, students, and adults. This book is used by parents, educators, and even managers in the workforce and is already a staple in many libraries. John Taylor Gatto's *Dumbing Us Down: The Hidden Curriculum of Compulsory Schooling* is another standard many homeschoolers point to as an articulation of some of the reasons they've decided to keep their children out of institutional schools.

Some contemporary homeschooling authors write from an unschooling perspective. Mary Griffith is one of the more prominent unschooling advocates. Her first book, *The Homeschooling Handbook,* takes a more general approach, but her second, *The Unschooling Handbook,* should be required reading for anyone seeking to unschool their children or better understand unschooling. Additionally, Griffith maintains a website (www.marygriffith.net/Site/homeschooling.html) and blog (http://virallearning.blogspot.com) that are packed with useful information about homeschooling in general and unschooling in particular. Grace Llewellyn, whose website is also a font of useful information (www.gracellewellyn.com), concentrates on unschooling teens in *The Teenage Liberation Handbook: How to Quit School and Get a Real Life and Education* and *Real Lives: Eleven Teenagers Who Don't Go to School Tell Their Own Stories.* Other writers and thinkers maintain blogs and websites and communicate via electronic discussion lists.

HOW LIBRARIES CAN BEST CONNECT WITH UNSCHOOLERS

Unschoolers are not the sort of people who come to library programs en masse, especially programs designed to teach something like library skills. But even though unschoolers may not be interested in formal library classes, they might welcome other opportunities to be involved in the library. They might be particularly interested in volunteering, advocating, or even joining the library staff as paid employees. In chapter 7 we explore some of the advantages of setting up a homeschooler-friendly volunteer program.

As a group, unschoolers use library collections extensively and may be some of a library's more obvious homeschooling patrons. As we see in chapter 7, connecting with this group can be a particular challenge, although one of the surest ways to make a good impression is through a good

PROFILE

Mary Griffith

When asked how she came to homeschooling, Mary Griffith replies, "The short and flip answer is 'I had kids.'" Like many homeschoolers and unschoolers, Griffith was a model pupil in school: she was well-behaved and got straight A's, but she was also bored. When she became a mother and started thinking about sending her older daughter, Kate, to school, "I couldn't stand the idea of her having to sit still in a classroom and get all that knowledge doled out to her in appropriate little bits, not to mention all that waiting around for the next thing. I figured if one was to be bored through large chunks of the day, one could at least be somewhere comfortable."

Mary Griffith began her family's homeschooling journey by doing a lot of reading with the kids and making sure that materials for learning and exploring were readily available: books, paper, pens, crayons, paints, blocks, Legos, and science toys. Most of their learning was informal, although, as the girls got older, Griffith and some other homeschooling families began a homeschooling Brownie troop, and she felt the family learned a lot doing badge work from *Try-Its for Brownie Girl Scouts*. Her younger daughter, Christie, went through a stage of wanting to be taught how to read more formally, but, bored and frustrated, they eventually abandoned the program and Christie learned to read on her own. Kate continued learning informally throughout her teen years until she went off to study drama in New York City. Christie, currently an NCAA fencer at Temple University, opted to do some more formal work in her teens to help her meet her goals as a collegiate athlete.

Griffith reports that she fell into writing about unschooling when Prima Publishing brought up the idea of writing a tradebook about homeschooling that eventually became *The Homeschooling Handbook*. After that, Mary Griffith wrote *The Unschooling Handbook* partially as "an antidote" to some of the school-like portions of her first book. Currently she's working on a book called *Viral Learning,* which promises to be an exploration of how homeschooling affects families and society in general.

old-fashioned reference transaction. Unschoolers are the ones who are likely to be looking for every last thing they can find on a topic or to have particular—and sometimes peculiar—interests. Often they want nothing more from a library than its collection and occasional assistance in finding what they need, although the multimedia subject kits described in chapter 9 are often particularly welcome in unschooling homes. Unschooling families can get excited about resources other families might resist such as online databases, pamphlet files, and microfilm, and it's easy to mention that these things exist through the course of your normal routine. Unschoolers also appreciate seeing the works of writers such as John Holt in your collection, and, like any other homeschooler, they appreciate seeing their perspective represented in homeschooling collections and materials.

3

Homeschooling for Religious Reasons: Conservative Protestants

Conservative Protestant homeschoolers have such a high profile in today's society that some people believe that all homeschoolers are conservative Protestants. Although one study suggested that 75 percent of homeschooling parents are conservative Protestants, the true number is difficult to gauge with any certainty.[1] Of homeschooling parents surveyed by the National Center for Education Statistics, 72 percent indicated that they were homeschooling to provide religious or moral instruction, although what type of religious or moral instruction they were providing is unclear.[2] Still, there is no doubt that conservative Protestants make up a large percentage of the homeschooling population and that, as sociologist Mitchell K. Stevens explores in his book *Kingdom of Children: Culture and Controversy in the Homeschooling Movement*, this group has a sizable and strong support network. Even so, be wary of stereotyping conservative Protestants. Although they may be united in some aspects of their faith, conservative Protestants don't necessarily agree on all issues, political or otherwise, and they certainly don't all homeschool in the same way. Some Protestants of strong faith who homeschool wouldn't consider themselves conservative at all. Although I discuss them as a group here, be assured that this community is not so easy to pin down.

RAYMOND AND DOROTHY MOORE

Any exploration of homeschooling's explosion in the conservative Protestant community should begin with educators Raymond and Dorothy Moore. Raymond Moore made his career as a teacher, administrator, and researcher. At the same time, his wife Dorothy worked as a teacher and researcher, often alongside her husband. After years of research and observation, the Moores came to the conclusion that Americans were pushing their children into formal education too young. In 1975 they published their first major book, *Better Late Than Early*, in which their core beliefs began to take shape: that children aren't ready for formal instruction until they are eight to ten years old, and that they learn best when they are doing real work. The Moores spent the ensuing years writing and speaking, honing their beliefs and trying to get homeschooling into the public consciousness.

At first blush, the Moores' beliefs don't sound too far off John Holt's unschooling philosophy, and they aren't. In fact, after some years of misunderstanding, the Moores and Holt developed a rapport. Like Holt, the Moores believed in some degree of child-led education and argued that children learn best when they follow their interests and engage in "real" work. Unlike Holt, though, the Moores emphasized the potential negative influence of peers and institutions on small children, particularly in the development of character. Eventually the Moores developed their three point "Moore Formula," an approach to homeschooling that they thought would guarantee any child a complete education: (1) study, but not too much, especially in the primary grades; (2) engage in manual labor, which is as important as, or even more important than, study; and (3) participate in service to one's family and the community. The Moores sought to spread their formula and support homeschooling families of all types through the creation of the Moore Foundation (www.moorefoundation.com), an organization that continues their work today.

Throughout their careers, Raymond and Dorothy Moore favored an ecumenical and inclusionary approach to education and homeschooling, but their Seventh-Day Adventist faith gave them legitimacy in conservative Protestant circles, especially after James Dobson interviewed Raymond on his *Focus on the Family* radio show in the early 1980s. A striking number of families who started homeschooling at that time cite Dobson's endorsement as a strong influence on their decision to homeschool. In fact, although the Moores don't have the kind of name recognition they once did, Dobson remains a powerful force in the conservative Protestant community and a vocal proponent of homeschooling.

WHY CONSERVATIVE PROTESTANTS HOMESCHOOL

Conservative Protestants don't all homeschool for the same reasons, but many of them consider faith and spiritual development to be an important part of educating their children. As Cathy Duffy notes in *100 Top Picks for Homeschool Curriculum,* "Everyone operates by one worldview or another. . . . A Christian worldview colors everything with the belief in God's existence."[3] This may be a concern for any Christian, but many conservative Protestants feel that it is important for their children's education to connect to their faith in meaningful ways. At the most basic, parents would like to ensure that prayer, Bible readings, and devotionals are part of their daily routines. Many parents also want a literal interpretation of the Bible to form the basis of their children's curriculum; this is perhaps most vividly expressed in concerns about evolution and creationism. Parents may also be dismayed at the secular humanism they see at the core of public school curriculums—the idea that the individual and not God is the ultimate authority.

Private Christian schools are an option for some families, but economic issues can make private schools prohibitive, particularly for large and single-income families. Some families who could afford private schools have concerns about the doctrinal leanings or academic quality of Christian schools in their area. As with other types of homeschoolers, conservative Protestants are also apt to appreciate the amount of quality time homeschooling allows families to spend together and the strong familial relationships this time encourages.

HOME SCHOOL LEGAL DEFENSE ASSOCIATION

In 1983, a time in which homeschooling was on the rise but still illegal or legally questionable in many states, homeschooling proponent Michael Farris formed the Home School Legal Defense Association (HSLDA). HSLDA is a conservative Protestant organization which, according to its mission, seeks "to defend and advance the constitutional right of parents to direct the education of their children."[4] Today the organization is one of the most powerful not only in the conservative Protestant homeschooling community but in the homeschooling community at large.

HSLDA was initially formed as a sort of insurance policy: membership guaranteed that, within certain parameters, the organization's lawyers would defend homeschooling families should legal action be taken against them. Through the years, HSLDA has expanded into a lobbying force that strives to control legislation that might impact homeschoolers. With thousands of members, the organization now supports a staff of more than fifty and has founded several other organizations and institutions with ties to homeschooling and conservative Protestantism, including Generation Joshua (www.generationjoshua.org), the Home School Foundation (www.homeschoolfoundation.org), and Patrick Henry College (www.phc.edu). HSLDA's website (www.hslda.org) is a font of information for homeschoolers, including homeschooling laws from state to state, pending legislation, and links to support groups in all fifty states. Any homeschooler can join HSLDA and reap its benefits, but many—including other Christians and even other conservative Protestants—choose not to join because they have concerns about the organization's involvement in politics or specifics of its conservative ideology.

VOICES IN CONSERVATIVE PROTESTANT HOMESCHOOLING

No discussion of homeschooling in the conservative Protestant community would be complete without mentioning Mary Pride. Mary Pride is a homeschooling mother, author, and the publisher of *Practical Homeschooling*, one of the more prominent homeschooling magazines on the market. Pride also maintains a website, Homeschool World (www.home-school.com), that serves as the official home for *Practical Homeschooling* as well as the newest incarnation of her famous *Big Book of Home Learning: Mary Pride's Complete Guide to Getting Started in Homeschooling*. Through the magazine, the site, and the guide, Pride offers homeschooling advice and reviews resources from a conservative Protestant perspective.

There are myriad other voices in the conservative Protestant homeschooling world. Homeschooling mother, author, and speaker Carol Barnier has made an impact on homeschoolers through her humorous approach to writing and talking about such topics as homeschooling easily distracted children, coping with daily life, and teaching reading. Her books include *If I'm Diapering a Watermelon, Then Where'd I Leave the Baby?* and *How to Get Your Child Off the Refrigerator and On to Learning*. Her

> **RESOURCES**
>
> *Homeschooling Magazines for Conservative Protestants*
>
> Home School Digest: http://www.homeschooldigest.com
> Homeschooling Today: http://www.homeschoolingtoday.com
> The Old Schoolhouse: http://www.thehomeschoolmagazine.com
> Practical Homeschooling: http://www.home-school.com/catalog/pages/phs.php3

website (www.opengifts.org) includes a biography, information about her books and speaking engagements (including audio excerpts from her speeches), and a section on teaching tips. There are dozens of writers and speakers like Barnier, experienced homeschoolers who have become experts on an aspect of homeschooling and found creative ways to share their knowledge. There are more magazines (see box above) and conferences for conservative Protestants than there are for any other type of homeschooler, and there are many opportunities for people with something to say.

CURRICULUMS

Many of the top names in homeschooling curriculums come from a conservative Protestant perspective. A Beka Book (www.abeka.com) began as a producer of textbooks for Christian schools and has evolved into a business that also caters to homeschoolers. It offers an accredited home study program as well as a host of textbooks and teaching aids used by Christian homeschoolers. Alpha Omega Publications (www.aop.com) is a producer that offers Christian-based curriculums in a variety of formats. KONOS (www.konos.com) offers packaged hands-on, multidisciplinary unit study plans that can be used with a variety of age levels at once, one of many ways parents choose to handle homeschooling larger families. Some other big names that provide curriculums, distance learning programs, and other learning materials are the Weaver Curriculum from Alpha Omega Publications, Bob Jones University Press (www.bjupress.com), and Advanced Training Institute International (http://ati.iblp.org). This is, truly, just the tip of the iceberg. One can find dozens of other options through a perusal of current homeschooling magazines, books, and websites.

HOW LIBRARIES CAN BEST CONNECT WITH CONSERVATIVE PROTESTANT HOMESCHOOLERS

Many librarians I have spoken with over the years are concerned that conservative Protestant homeschoolers might be inclined to challenge library materials in a concerted way. In my experience, conservative Protestant homeschoolers are no more or less likely to express concerns about materials than any other group of parents or even the population at large. In any case, avoiding contact with this population is no way to ensure that the library's collection won't be challenged. Like anyone who visits the library, conservative Protestant homeschoolers are primarily there to locate materials that serve their needs. When they find the types of materials they're looking for, they leave the library happy.

A real problem is that many libraries simply are not stocking enough Christian-focused materials to meet potential demand. Conservative Protestants and other Christians are a sizable segment of the U.S. population. In a recent issue of *Publisher's Weekly*, publisher Jonathan Merkh suggests that the only reason more overtly Christian titles aren't showing up on bestseller lists is that those lists don't factor in sales at Christian bookstores.[5] Where demand warrants, developing and effectively marketing a strong collection of materials that address Christian beliefs and lifestyles benefit the library, conservative Protestant homeschoolers, and the community as a whole.

NOTES

1. Yi Cai, Johnmarshall Reeve, and Dawn T. Robinson, "Home Schooling and Teaching Style: Comparing the Motivating Styles of Home School and Public School Teachers," *Journal of Educational Psychology* 94, no. 2 (2002): 372–80.
2. Daniel Princiotta and Stacey Bielick, *Homeschooling in the United States: 2003* (Washington, DC: National Center for Education Statistics, 2005), 13.
3. Cathy Duffy, *100 Top Picks for Homeschool Curriculum: Choosing the Right Curriculum and Approach for Your Child's Learning Style* (Nashville, TN: Broadman and Holman, 2005), 59.
4. "About HSLDA," http://www.hslda.org/about/default.asp (accessed May 28, 2007).
5. Jonathan Merkh, "Jesus and the Bestseller List: What Would Jesus Count?" *Publisher's Weekly*, April 3, 2006, 80.

4

Homeschooling for Religious Reasons: Other Religions

The Protestant Christian homeschoolers discussed in chapter 3 are a visible and vocal segment of the population, but not all those who homeschool for religious reasons are conservative Protestants. There are no reliable statistical data to give us an idea of their numbers, but there are a significant number of Catholics, Jews, Muslims, and members of other faiths who homeschool, and each group has its own needs. These families homeschool for many of the same reasons conservative Protestants homeschool: they believe that homeschooling fosters and strengthens family bonds; they are dissatisfied with available public and private schools; private religious schools are unavailable or too expensive; or they fear religious persecution in public schools. Libraries' traditional mission to provide a balanced collection in a nonjudgmental environment serves these families well, but librarians can go further to understand these homeschoolers' particular concerns, challenges, and resources.

CATHOLIC HOMESCHOOLERS

It's hard to say why Catholic homeschoolers are not as visible as other Christian homeschoolers. Catholic homeschoolers have an increasingly strong presence in most communities, with relatively well-developed support systems and an abundance of specialized product and curriculum options (see box on page 29). Like other homeschoolers, Catholics choose to teach their children at home for any number of reasons. Some express dissatisfaction with the current parochial school system, citing such issues as the presence of sex education, the quality of religious instruction, the use of secular textbooks, and poor academic standards. Some Catholic homeschoolers seek to maintain family time, and others simply believe that the best place to receive a high-quality education is at home. A large number of Catholic homeschoolers choose a classical or Charlotte Mason approach to homeschooling, and many Catholics consider themselves eclectic homeschoolers (see more on these philosophies in chapter 6).

The largest national organization for homeschoolers is Traditions of Roman Catholic Homes, or T.O.R.C.H. (www.catholic-homeschool.com). T.O.R.C.H.'s primary mission is to support homeschooling families. It has a newsletter, encourages the formation of local support groups, and sponsors leadership conferences. Another group of potential interest is the National Association of Catholic Homes and Educators (NACHE: www.nache.org). This is an organization aimed at all Catholic parents, but it pays particular attention to homeschoolers' needs in its quarterly journal, *The Catholic Home*, and its annual Catholic Family Expo.

Heart and Mind: A Resource for Catholic Homeschoolers, a relatively new quarterly publication that began printing in 2004, addresses the "how-to's" of Catholic homeschooling with regular columns on classical education, thrifty homeschooling, homeschooling children with special needs, literature, and product reviews. The Heart and Mind website (www.heart-and-mind.com) is an excellent resource for regional conference information and carefully selected links to websites of interest to Catholic homeschoolers. This publication is particularly notable for its easygoing and practical approach.

> **PROFILE**

Maureen Wittmann

When Maureen Wittmann was in the eighth grade, back surgery kept her out of school for six months. With only an hour or two of tutoring each schoolday, Wittmann was able to keep up with her fellow students. If she started to get ahead, the school would ask the tutor to slow down and hold her back. This had a huge impact on Wittmann: "I resented that I had to spend seven hours in a school building, when I knew that I could receive a quality education at home in just two hours." When she befriended a homeschool graduate in college, she knew she wanted to homeschool her own children someday.

Today Wittmann is homeschooling her seven children—the youngest still a preschooler and the eldest starting to look at college options. A devout Catholic, Wittmann believes that faith and learning are intertwined. She puts it like this: "We are made in God's image. Let's think about that for a moment. What does God do? He creates. He created us and the earth. Therefore, it is only natural that we have a desire to create. It feels good to create, to learn, to explore, to discover. I try, as a parent and homeschooler, to take advantage of these natural tendencies in my children." Rather than follow a rigid program, Wittmann has opted for individualized instruction with her children, giving each a say in their studies. She emphasizes the use of "real books" over textbooks and has developed several creative ways to ensure that every child gets what he or she needs, including hiring the older children to tutor the younger.

In addition to homeschooling, Maureen Wittmann is a writer and speaker at homeschooling conferences. She has coedited two books with Rachel Mackson: *A Catholic Homeschool Treasury: Nurturing Children's Love for Learning* and *The Catholic Homeschool Companion.* She is the author of *For the Love of Literature* (about incorporating real books into a homeschooling program) and is currently at work on a book about teens, *No Question Left Behind.* A contributing editor to Heart and Mind (www.heart-and-mind.com), she also blogs (http://maureenwittmann.blogspot.com), maintains a website (www.catholictreasury.com), moderates a few Yahoo groups, and recently started a monthly column at CatholicMom.com.

RESOURCES

Selected Curriculum Options for Catholic Homeschoolers

Seton Home Study School: http://www.setonhome.org

> This correspondence school began as a brick-and-mortar school in Manassas, Virginia, for families who wanted more control over their children's Catholic education. It now offers books, workbooks, lesson plans, tests, a grading service, and academic counselors for children in grades K–12.

Our Lady of the Rosary School: http://www.olrs.com

> This organization seeks to make curriculum and learning materials based on Catholic doctrine available internationally. It offers a correspondence program as well as complete curriculums that parents can administer themselves for children in preschool through grade 12.

Mother of Divine Grace School: http://www.motherofdivinegrace.org

> This organization offers a classically based Catholic correspondence program and support materials for homeschooling families with children in grades K–12.

Our Lady of Victory: http://www.olvs.org

> This organization offers correspondence courses as well as curriculums for grades K–12 based on traditional Catholic teachings with a secondary focus on church history.

Catholic Heritage Curricula: http://www.chcweb.com

> This organization provides a wide array of home learning materials for children in preschool through grade 12 and encourages a "gentle" approach to education.

Kolbe Academy: http://www.kolbe.org

> This correspondence school for children in grades K–12 is founded on the Ignatian method, a teaching method based on the writings of St. Ignatius of Loyola that encourages reasoning over memorization.

PAGAN HOMESCHOOLERS

Many Pagans choose to homeschool for academic and social as well as religious reasons. As a frequently maligned and misunderstood minority, some Pagans prefer to maintain a low profile. Because of this, Pagans can be an unrecognized and underserved segment of the homeschooling community as well as the community at large. There aren't a great number of resources available for Pagan homeschoolers. *Pagan Homeschooling* by Kristin Madden is an essential title for any library serving a Pagan community of any size. Goddess Moon Circles Academy (www.goddess moon.org/education/goddess_moon_circles_academy.htm) is a site to watch, since it offers a pioneering Pagan-based correspondence school for children up through grade 12. Pagan homeschoolers utilize materials on any number of subjects, so librarians serve them best with a balanced collection and open mind. The exploration and appreciation of nature are an integral part of the Pagan faith system, so books about nature—particularly local flora and fauna—can be of particular interest, along with books that explore world religions and mythologies.

JEWISH HOMESCHOOLERS

Although there seem to be a fair number of Jewish homeschoolers in the United States, there are relatively few organizations and publications created with them in mind. A great number of families choose to unschool, create their own curriculums, or use available secular curriculum packages. Families who are particularly concerned about religious instruction send their children to religious classes on a part-time basis or create their own course of home study. The Shluchim Office recently opened the first online Jewish school (www.shluchim.org/main/inside.asp?id=1416), but it remains to be seen how much of an impact this has in the Jewish homeschooling community at large.

OTHER GROUPS

One sees evidence on the Internet and hears of people of many other faiths—Muslims, Hindus, Buddhists, Jehovah's Witnesses, Mormons, Quakers—who homeschool, but there is little formal support available to address their particular needs. Most libraries don't serve such a wide array of homeschoolers, but at the same time librarians should be aware

PROFILE

Kristin Madden

When Kristin Madden and her family moved from Connecticut to New Mexico, she knew that the public school system was lacking, and she was ready to consider private schools when her then preschool-age son was ready to start kindergarten. She didn't consider homeschooling, though, until repeated instances of neglect and violence forced her to pull her son out of his day-care facility, the "best" in the area by all accounts. While mulling over the family's next step, Madden began exploring homeschooling. She and her son tried it, loved it, and have been homeschooling ever since.

A Druid, dean of Ardantane's School of Shamanic Studies, and author of the book *Pagan Homeschooling,* Madden says that a lot of Pagan homeschoolers stay "in the closet" and that there are more Pagans homeschooling than casual observers might suspect. She also says that, although most Pagans don't homeschool for religious reasons, "Like people of other faiths, our spirituality informs our experience of life in every way." She finds that matters of faith often naturally lead to academic subjects, and vice versa.

Madden and her son, now eleven, are eclectic homeschoolers, working with a combination of unschooling and school-at-home techniques. They homeschool year-round and embrace learning opportunities as they arise, as when Madden's son accompanies her on book tours. While developing a curriculum for her son, Madden, already a prolific author, realized that Pagan homeschoolers lacked a book that addressed their particular needs and concerns, so she wrote one. She is currently at work on another homeschooling book—this one from a secular perspective—and has thoughts of writing a companion volume to *Pagan Homeschooling.* For up-to-date information on Kristin Madden's writings, speaking engagements, and other activities, visit her online at www.kristinmadden.com.

that they might be surprised at the number of faiths practiced by homeschoolers in their communities. They should also be aware if they have an enclave of a particular type of homeschooler in their communities and purchase resources accordingly. Most faith-based materials serve homeschoolers and non-homeschoolers alike.

RESOURCES

Selected Electronic Discussion Lists for Religious Homeschoolers

Bahai Homeschooling (Baha'i): http://groups.yahoo.com/group/bahai_homeschooling/

Buddhist Homeschoolers: http://groups.yahoo.com/group/Buddhist-homeschool/

HUUH-L, Homeschooling Unitarian Universalists Humanists and Those on Other Roads Less Traveled: http://lists.uua.org/mailman/listinfo/huuh-l/

Jehovah's Witness Homeschool: http://groups.yahoo.com/group/Jehovahs_Witness-homeschool/

Muslim Homeschool: http://groups.yahoo.com/group/Muslim_Homeschool/

Muslimhsers, Education for Muslim Children: http://groups.yahoo.com/group/muslimhsers/

Quaker Homeschooling Circle (QHC): http://lists.topica.com/lists/quakerhomeschool/

UUHomeschoolers (Unitarian Universalists): http://groups.yahoo.com/group/uuhomeschoolers/

5
Homeschooling Youth with Special Needs

Most families who have children who fall outside expected developmental timetables experience some level of frustration in their dealings with the institutional environments not only of schools but also of the medical and mental health communities. Having a child who has special needs—be they physical, mental, emotional, or some combination thereof—may be a challenge long before the child is officially diagnosed (if the child is ever diagnosed), and parents often find themselves compelled to develop strong advocacy skills to ensure their children's needs are being met. Many parents are most comfortable operating within institutional frameworks, but more and more exasperated parents are choosing to teach their children with special needs at home.

For the purposes of this chapter, "children with special needs" covers children who are dealing with any of a wide range of issues that require accommodation in learning and other environments. Parents most commonly choose to homeschool children who have learning disabilities, developmental disabilities, giftedness, and mental health issues. Many also homeschool children who are twice exceptional, meaning that they have learning disabilities in some areas and giftedness in others. Some parents opt to homeschool children dealing with temporary or more permanent medical issues, such as children waiting for an organ transplant or those with life-threatening allergies.

Talking about these children as a group can be somewhat misleading, since they have such a great variety of needs. Still, they are similar in that their unusual situations can compel people to question their expectations and assumptions about education and child development. Sometimes these questions lead families to homeschooling. In other cases, homeschooling parents discover their children's differences and challenges after they're already on the homeschooling path. Perhaps more so than for any other group, homeschooling for families with children with special needs can be as much a matter of practicality and necessity as it is of philosophy.

RATIONALES

Families who homeschool children with special needs are resting on assumptions that guide many of today's standard educational practices. There is some debate among researchers on issues involving class size and its impact on student achievement, but conventional wisdom in the community of professional educators maintains that students learn best and achieve more in classrooms with fewer students and more one-on-one interaction with teachers. The special education community has likewise embraced this idea, and many children who have learning disabilities and mental health issues are placed in environments with smaller student-adult ratios. The same applies to programs designed for gifted students, which also often rely on more flexible and student-led learning experiences that operate much like prevailing homeschooling methods. Parents point out that most institutional schools cannot provide the student-teacher ratio that the family can provide at home, and at least one study has suggested that homeschooling parents can provide their children with more academic engaged time than teachers in public schools.[1]

Most homeschooling parents feel that their ability to tailor instruction to their children's particular needs is one of the main benefits of homeschooling any child, but such flexibility may be even more important for children with less typical needs. Rather than force a child to adapt to the school's schedule, for instance, homeschoolers are free to adapt to the child's. Children who have particular environmental needs or suffer from attention issues can often be more easily accommodated in the relatively controlled environment of the home. Parents feel that their intimate knowledge of their children helps them create learning experiences that produce the best results.

Given the prevalence of public concern over the socialization of homeschooled children, it is somewhat ironic that many parents who have homeschooled children with special needs feel that homeschooling has given their children more positive social experiences than they would have had in institutional schools. Children who may have been socially isolated or bullied in institutional schools because of their labels and differences aren't made to suffer in homeschooling environments where they are accepted for who they are. In fact, many parents cite caustic social environments as one of the reasons they chose to homeschool in the first place. Far from isolating their children, most parents homeschooling children who have special needs go through the same efforts other homeschoolers do to provide their children with a variety of socialization experiences that include specialized classes and lessons, activities with homeschooling groups, church involvement, and participation in various community groups.

PHILOSOPHICAL AND CURRICULAR OPTIONS

Families who homeschool children with special needs can subscribe to any of the philosophies and methods discussed throughout this book. Conversely, they may be homeschooling because they see no other choice. Because children and families are so different and have such a wide variety of needs, there are no easy answers when it comes to the choice of curriculum or philosophy. Many families become eclectic homeschoolers, exploring and employing several methods and approaches in an attempt to find the combination that works best for their particular situation.

Books about homeschooling children with special needs recommend taking time to assess children's learning styles, interests, strengths, and weaknesses. In *Homeschooling the Challenging Child: A Practical Guide*, author and homeschooling mother Christine M. Field even recommends creating an Individualized Education Plan (IEP) similar to what a school would use when designing a curriculum for children with special needs. In *Creative Homeschooling: A Resource Guide for Smart Families*, Lisa Rivero advises parents to be cautious, flexible, and patient when designing a homeschooling program for children who are gifted or twice exceptional. Cathy Duffy's homeschool curriculum reviews in *100 Top Picks for Homeschool Curriculum* and on her website (www.cathyduffyreviews.com) can be particularly helpful for parents of children with special needs since she pays particular attention to how resources work for different teaching and learning styles. Librarians can help families by making these resources available along with other library resources that deal with issues involving children who have special needs.

RESOURCES

Selected Electronic Discussion Lists for Families Homeschooling Children with Special Needs

Homeschooling Special Needs Kidz: http://groups.yahoo.com/group/Homeschool_SpecialNeedsKidz/

> This busy electronic discussion list is for parents homeschooling children who have any type of special need.

Homeschooling Extraordinary Kids: Thinking Outside the Box: http://groups.yahoo.com/group/homeschoolingextraordinarykids/

> This electronic discussion list focuses on homeschooling children who have learning disabilities, giftedness, or some combination of the two. It encourages the sharing of resources and ideas for creating specialized learning programs and materials.

Special Needs Homeschool: Home Schooling Special Needs Children: http://groups.yahoo.com/group/special-needs-homeschool/

> This list focuses on families who are homeschooling at least one child with special needs, many of whom are medically fragile.

OTHER CONSIDERATIONS

Because of various laws that address the education of children with special needs—particularly learning and developmental disabilities—school districts provide screening, diagnostic, and support services for children, depending on the area of concern, from preschool through high school graduation. Different districts provide different levels of service, and districts from state to state and community to community vary widely in their policies regarding homeschoolers' access to these services. This becomes a major issue if, say, a child needs a service like occupational therapy. On a private basis, professional therapies can be tremendously expensive, and many health insurance policies cover them only minimally or not at all. Homeschoolers have to decide if they're going to try to deal with their children's issues on their own, pay out of pocket to work with a professional outside the school system, or attempt to utilize school

PROFILE

Lenore Colacion Hayes

Lenore Colacion Hayes and her husband began to worry about their son Nigel when it became apparent that he was having difficulty adjusting to institutional preschool environments. They consulted with their pediatrician and a psychologist. Both agreed that Nigel was healthy, spirited, and intelligent. They couldn't offer a diagnosis, but the psychologist warned the family that Nigel wouldn't fit well in an institutional school setting, so instead of sending Nigel off to kindergarten in 1989, the family started homeschooling.

Years later, when Nigel was ten or eleven, the Hayes family would learn that his issues had a name: Asperger's syndrome, a condition that wasn't even listed in the *Diagnostic Statistical Manual* in 1989. When they began homeschooling, they decided the best way to work with Nigel's uniqueness would be to forgo a formal curriculum and instead design learning experiences that focused on his strengths, weaknesses, and interests—a system very like unit studies. For example, when Nigel was six, he loved trains and Thomas the Tank Engine. They read a lot of books about trains. Lenore and Nigel also worked on math skills with a set of train manipulatives purchased from a local teacher supply store, and she arranged an outing for Nigel on a real train. "It was a matter of my husband and I breaking out of what we thought we knew about education and learning," says Hayes. She found Howard Gardner's theories on multiple intelligences helpful when considering Nigel's learning style and eventually concluded that Nigel worked best when he wrestled with things alone and had someone available to consult when he had questions.

When Hayes began homeschooling, there wasn't much in the way of support. There was one homeschooling group in the area at that time, although through the years she saw many homeschooling groups come and go. Homeschooling Nigel got easier as he got older, too, because he was "so motivated to sit and read." The library was always a vital part of their homeschooling lives. At the beginning, they didn't have a lot of money, so they would get the Chinaberry catalog, read through to find books of interest, and then get them from the public library to have a look. If Nigel really loved something, Hayes would purchase it. They had a library within walking distance, although they

> visited other branches as well. Libraries are "a great equalizer," says Hayes. "They didn't seem to care that Nigel was odd."
>
> In 2002, Lenore Hayes published *Homeschooling the Child with ADD (or Other Special Needs),* and around the same time Nigel moved from homeschooling into adulthood. Today he frequents an area library known for its nonfiction video collection, and his interest in the library and the collection has been the basis of a friendship with one of the librarians. The family remains avid readers, and Hayes retains her interest in homeschooling. When asked what libraries can do to welcome homeschoolers, she suggests the kinds of things many homeschoolers talk about: building good collections of nonfiction DVDs, opening up meeting rooms to homeschooling organizations, and running reading incentive programs throughout the year. She says that homeschoolers can be reluctant to approach library staff with requests because "you don't want to be viewed as being a problem," but she also notes that most homeschoolers are immensely grateful to the public library for the services they already offer. Overall, Hayes says, homeschoolers are looking for services that are self-directed, along with many things most libraries already have.

services. Other homeschooling families who suspect that their children have special needs choose not to pursue an official diagnosis either because it seems irrelevant or because they worry about the potential consequences of a label. In any case, it's not unusual to have a homeschooling parent visit the library on a quest for professional literature on various aspects of teaching and working with children who have special needs. Many do this before they make the decision to homeschool in the first place.

HOW LIBRARIES CAN BEST CONNECT WITH FAMILIES WHO HAVE CHILDREN WITH SPECIAL NEEDS

Most public libraries make efforts to ensure that their materials, programs, services, and facilities are accessible and welcoming to people with a wide range of skills, abilities, and issues. Reaching out to the potentially underserved and those who could benefit most from our services is a core value

PROFILE

Catherine Arnott Smith

Catherine Arnott Smith, homeschooling mom and assistant professor in the School of Library and Information Studies at the University of Wisconsin–Madison, first began considering homeschooling when she was a doctoral student and her son was still a preschooler. Through her teaching assistant position, she met an army doctor who, with his wife, was homeschooling their four children. Meanwhile, her son Simon was identified as profoundly gifted. His development as a toddler was uneven, and by first grade he was well matched with his age-level peers socially and in language arts but tested five grades ahead in math.

When Simon was in second grade, Smith finished her doctoral work and the family was getting ready to move. All the schools they researched wanted to either leave Simon with his age mates with no accommodation for his advanced math skills or move him ahead several grades, which would likely leave him behind socially and potentially frustrated in his reading and writing. As Smith says, "It just seemed ridiculous that we'd have to choose between educating the kid and letting him be happy with friends in a classroom."

Once they decided to homeschool, the family favored an eclectic approach, mixing textbooks, online learning, and unstructured time to allow Simon to pursue his interests. "At the beginning," Smith says, "I did not really know there *were* competing or even different philosophies." She has found that prevalent stereotypes about homeschoolers don't capture the reality of homeschooling, noting that in her experience most homeschoolers don't re-create school at home or unschool entirely, most "fall somewhere between those two extremes, and may even move back and forth depending on what the child needs and is ready for."

After four years of homeschooling, it became increasingly clear that Simon's interests and abilities in science were growing beyond the education the family could easily provide at home: "Science was easy to do when science meant growing beans in a jelly jar, but as science started to mean biology, and chemistry . . . it is really, really hard to do those without a lab." The Smiths also began having a more

> difficult time organizing meaningful academic discussions and activities with other homeschooled kids who were Simon's age and shared his interests and abilities. After much thought, they enrolled Simon in a private Catholic high school, where he is two grade levels ahead of other children his age. Some of his classes are more challenging than others, but for now he wants to stick with it. When asked why, he responds, "I just know I do."
>
> "What can I say?" says Catherine Smith. "He's almost thirteen."

of public libraries, and it is a matter of philosophy to most librarians. The first step toward serving homeschooling families with children who have special needs is to examine how your library is serving the special needs population in general. It goes without saying that libraries should be in compliance with federal, state, and local laws governing accessible design. Beyond that, libraries should look to the spirit of these laws to make doorways, bathrooms, aisles, furniture, and equipment as welcoming, flexible, and adaptable as possible. If physical design issues prevent families from using the library, it makes other considerations moot.

There are other things many libraries already do that serve this population—along with homeschoolers in general and any number of other people who walk in the door. Often the challenge is to figure out the best ways to reach out and let people know what's available. Part of that is learning how to talk to people with special needs. Read up on disabilities, learn about "people first" language, and explore alternative means of communication and matters of etiquette. Consider looking for outside training opportunities or perhaps setting up an in-service training day designed to help staff become more aware of people with disabilities and learn the best ways to work with them.

These are the skills that help librarians connect families with materials that may be of particular interest—things like large print books, high/low books, audio productions, music, films, games, and multimedia kits. Parents of children with special needs may also be looking for materials pertaining to those needs in consumer health and parenting collections. They may need referrals to more specialized libraries and collections. Library staff should also be aware of and keep resource information available on local organizations and programs that assist those with special needs and their families. Examples include support groups, the National

Library Service for the Blind and Physically Handicapped, and local radio reading programs.

Again, the challenge of serving homeschoolers with special needs is the same as serving anyone with special needs: let people know they're welcome, have a variety of materials available, and be knowledgeable and ready to connect people with the resources they need. Since librarians strive to be experts at connecting people with information, this is an area in which most libraries can easily excel.

NOTE

1. D. Lawrence Ward, "An Exploratory Study of Home School Instructional Environments and Their Effects on the Basic Skills of Students with Learning Disabilities," *Education and Treatment of Children* 20, no. 2 (1997): 150–73.

6

Other Homeschooling Groups and Trends

In previous chapters we explore the more dominant philosophies and issues in homeschooling, but there are some smaller movements and ideas worth including, if only to give readers more evidence of the infinite variety one can encounter in the homeschooling world. Homeschoolers who are part of the groups mentioned in this chapter almost always subscribe to more than one philosophy. A military homeschooler, for example, may very well be a conservative Protestant who unschools. Remember: it is dangerous to make broad generalizations. The homeschooling community is fluid, and few families fit into one neat category. These groups are also some of the smallest in the homeschooling world, so they are the ones librarians are the least likely to see. Their rareness makes them all the more interesting.

HOMESCHOOLING UNDER THE RADAR

When the homeschooling movement first began in the 1970s and '80s, most people who knew anything about homeschooling knew that some families homeschooled in secret in areas where homeschooling was illegal or the laws governing homeschooling were especially cumbersome. Homeschooling is legal in all fifty states today, so homeschoolers who choose not to follow applicable laws do so for other reasons—because they think the legal obligations are unfair, perhaps, or because they aren't comfortable reporting to any type of government entity. In any case, there are fewer people homeschooling under the radar than there once were, but it's worth noting that these families still exist. This is one of the reasons homeschooling groups can be extremely concerned about privacy and one of the reasons librarians should be sure to educate homeschoolers about libraries' commitment to confidentiality.

CHARLOTTE MASON HOMESCHOOLERS

Charlotte Mason was a nineteenth-century British educator who advocated a gentle and empathetic approach to teaching elementary school-age children. To get the full thrust of Mason's educational philosophies, one could explore the six volumes she wrote on the subject, although a fair number of homeschoolers who follow her teachings probably haven't. Some of Mason's ideas have become such a normal part of the educational landscape that many homeschoolers—and even institutional educators—incorporate them into their teaching without being completely aware of it.

Mason's ideas were centered on developing a solid character and good habits. She argued that children need short, focused lessons along with plenty of exercise and exposure to nature. She rejected textbooks in favor of primary sources and great works of literature in their entirety, and she recommended the benefits of time spent with great works of art. A devout Christian, for Mason spiritual and moral development were just as important as academic development, so she required her teachers to include prayer and Bible readings in their daily routines.

Today Mason's ideas are embraced in various segments of the homeschooling community. Her emphasis on character development and daily Bible readings makes her methods popular among Christians. Her ideas about nature study and art appreciation resonate with many unschoolers and eclectic homeschoolers. Respect for children and their individuality is a strong belief throughout the homeschooling world. Some homeschoolers follow Mason's ideas more literally, and several books have been written on the subject. Susan Schaeffer Macaulay is often credited with introducing Mason's ideas to the homeschooling world in 1984 with *For the Children's Sake: Foundations of Education for Home and School*. She inspired homeschooling advocate Karen Andreola, whose *A Charlotte Mason Companion: Personal Reflections on the Gentle Art of Learning* and website (www.charlottemason.com) provide a wealth of information about applying Mason's ideas to homeschooling. Catherine Levinson gives a more compact view of Mason's approach in *A Charlotte Mason*

Education: A Home Schooling How-To Manual. Additionally, *When Children Love to Learn: A Practical Application of Charlotte Mason's Philosophy for Today,* edited by Elaine Cooper, takes a more philosophical and academic approach to using Mason's ideas in the home. Charlotte Mason homeschoolers may come to the library looking for her writings and may also be interested in readers' advisory services to locate the best literature to use with their children and teens. With Mason's emphasis on art, this population would also be particularly interested in art print collections where they're available.

CLASSICAL HOMESCHOOLERS

Classical homeschoolers follow a highly structured approach best articulated in Susan Wise Bauer and Jessie Wise's *The Well-Trained Mind.* Based on the medieval trivium, classical homeschoolers divide learning into three stages: grammar/memorization (grades K–4), logic (grades 5–8), and rhetoric (grades 9–12). The method emphasizes learning through language and seeks to develop discipline, virtue, and logical thinking. Proponents of classical homeschooling focus on the study of history and great books, including epics, legends, mythology, poetry, and ultimately primary sources. Math, hard sciences, and the arts are also part of the classical curriculum. The method is used by secular homeschoolers, but it presupposes a Christian worldview and is utilized by Christians of all types. Classical homeschoolers are focused on solid academics and large amounts of reading, which makes classical homeschoolers particular library fans. Librarians enjoy these homeschoolers' attention to some of the library's less popular holdings of high quality and literary merit.

MONTESSORI HOMESCHOOLERS

Early twentieth-century Italian educator Maria Montessori's ideas have formed the basis of several preschool and elementary school programs throughout the United States, so most librarians are probably at least casually acquainted with Montessori philosophy. Basically, Montessori believed that teachers should create a "prepared environment" and then act as unobtrusive guides to children's exploration of that environment and the learning materials found therein. Montessori argued that children learn best through the use of targeted hands-on manipulatives and

> **PROFILE**
>
> ## *Jessica DeFore*
>
> Jessica DeFore and her husband knew that the public schools in their county were less than ideal. When their daughter Camille was old enough to attend school, they opted to pay $500 per year and provide their own transportation to send her to better schools in a neighboring county, a 160-mile round-trip. In addition to the car ride, Camille was getting a half-hour or hour's worth of homework each night, which "left little time for being five years old between homework, dinner, and bedtime." The final straw came when the school taught the children, even kindergarteners, a chant about standardized tests. DeFore recalls that "Camille would come home chanting and brought home order forms for purchasing a T-shirt that is meant to inspire children, along with a permission form for her to participate in a parade around the school to celebrate taking the CRCT test." DeFore and her husband decided their money could be put to better use and began to explore homeschooling.
>
> DeFore started reading about homeschooling in December of Camille's kindergarten year, and the family officially began homeschooling the following September. She read extensively from books like Cathy Duffy's *100 Top Picks for Homeschool Curriculum* to determine her teaching style and Camille's learning style, which eventually led her to *The Well-Trained Mind* and classical approach. At the end of Camille's first-grade year, homeschooling has been an enjoyable success: "We've read books we wouldn't have thought to read or had time for: *The Complete Tales of Winnie-the-Pooh, A Bear Called Paddington, Charlotte's Web,* and other long chapter books that are pushed to the side for glossy Disney Princess books and other heavily advertised books that have almost zero literary and moral value."
>
> Now that her daughter is homeschooling, DeFore is amazed at how much of Camille's development she and her husband had been leaving to strangers and peers when they were sending Camille to school. Since Camille is still young, she is in the grammar stage of the classical program, which means a lot of memorization. DeFore notes that many people think of the classical curriculum as rigorous—"which we are, but we utilize what the child is ready for; we would never push our children beyond what they are capable of accomplishing. What

> you may consider rigorous at first becomes second nature to a child who has been exposed to healthy, positive attitudes about learning." Now the family is eagerly looking forward to the day their younger son, Danny, is ready to start his homeschooling program.

real-world work, and she believed that traditional curriculums were countering rather than supporting student achievement. Most Montessori schools, and by extension Montessori homeschoolers, don't necessarily follow Montessori's ideas to the letter, but they do utilize key elements of her theories, which are fully explained in her many published writings and speeches. For more information on how the Montessori method can be applied to homeschooling, visit the International Montessori Index at www.montessori.edu.

AFRICAN AMERICAN HOMESCHOOLERS

According to the National Center for Education Statistics, 9.4 percent of the homeschooling population identified themselves as black in 2003.[1] There have always been African American homeschoolers, but, along with the rest of the homeschooling population, they've become a more visible and active presence in recent years. Several organizations and publications are geared toward African American homeschoolers, and they're getting more attention in the media. This is a group whose members homeschool for myriad reasons, sometimes reasons tied to race and sometimes not. In her book *Morning by Morning: How We Home-Schooled Our African-American Sons to the Ivy League,* Paula Penn-Nabrit talks about the events that finally led her and her husband to decide to homeschool their three sons. Her family's story provides a great deal of insight into some of the reasons African American families homeschool, although even Penn-Nabrit says that it's not the choice for everyone. As with so many other groups, libraries best serve African American homeschoolers when they first work to serve people as individuals—in this case, particularly, by ensuring that the library is not participating in the kind of institutionalized racism that might have caused some families to give up on schools in the first place.

PROFILE

Paula Penn-Nabrit

When Paula Penn-Nabrit and her husband C. Madison decided to start homeschooling their three sons, twins Charles and Damon were in sixth grade and their younger brother Evan was in fourth. The products of preparatory schools and top-notch universities themselves, Penn-Nabrit and her husband initially tried to ensure their children's future educational opportunities by sending them to prep school. The family had experienced institutionalized racism and other problems in schools throughout the boys' youth, but they had attempted in each environment to work with the institution and be agents of positive change. An incident with their last school finally brought things to a head and made them reconsider what was going to be best for their sons in the long term.

Says Penn-Nabrit, "Our homeschooling adventure actually began as a God-given vision." Throughout their experiences in institutional schools, she had become increasingly concerned about how teachers' and administrators' attitudes and assumptions were impacting their treatment of her children and her children's overall well-being. She wanted her sons to be "nurtured and validated holistically, i.e., spiritually, intellectually, and physically." She and her husband prayed and looked to scripture and their own educational backgrounds to build a curriculum that focused on this vision.

When asked about writers and thinkers who have influenced her ideas about homeschooling, Penn-Nabrit cites Proverbs 4:7: "Wisdom is the principal thing; therefore get wisdom: and with all thy getting get understanding." Penn-Nabrit and her husband ultimately designed a focused curriculum for their sons that emphasized depth and understanding. Because the boys were able to take time to focus, she reports, "we were able to challenge them at increasingly deeper and deeper levels as we worked with the same texts over a series of years." Texts they studied included the Bible, the holy writings of other religions, the *Odyssey,* and Shakespeare's plays.

The public library was a positive part of the family's homeschooling experience. According to Penn-Nabrit, her sons were comfortable in the library, and the librarians they worked with were interested and excited about their sons' academic endeavors right through their teen years. "As trite as it sounds, children really do live what they learn, and in the Columbus Metropolitan Library system our sons learned they were welcome in the public square of learning, academic discourse, and discovery. That seems like such an easily accessible thing in a capitalist democracy, but regrettably it is not. Its rarity made it all the more precious and valuable to our family."

It is equally rare to find a homeschooler who will tell you that her children hated homeschooling, but Penn-Nabrit is one who will. Her sons railed against homeschooling for years, even as they worked hard and made progress. "Unlike many other children who leave traditional academic environments to pursue homeschooling, our guys liked school." Still, Penn-Nabrit and her husband kept their faith. Leaving the rigid school environment gave the boys opportunities to volunteer, to be tutored, and to travel with their self-employed parents. In the end, the family was rewarded when all three boys were accepted to major universities—the twins at Princeton and Evan at Amherst College. Today Charles, Damon, and Evan are adults, and Paula Penn-Nabrit is, among other things, an active writer and speaker. To learn more about her and her family's experience with homeschooling, read her book, *Morning by Morning: How We Home-Schooled Our African-American Sons to the Ivy League,* or visit her website at www.paula penn-nabrit.com.

MILITARY HOMESCHOOLERS

Families in which a parent is an active member of the military live relatively unusual lifestyles. Families may end up moving around the country, even internationally, frequently and sometimes unexpectedly. Some military families homeschool for one or more of the many reasons or philosophies explored throughout this book. Others homeschool in direct response to their lifestyle and frequent moves. Homeschooling can provide more educational continuity than children might obtain when continually facing new schools and curriculums, and homeschooling can be a temporary solution when families find themselves dissatisfied with institutional schools in a particular area. Legal issues can be a particular concern for

> **RESOURCES**
>
> ## Websites of Interest to African American Homeschoolers
>
> African American Homeschoolers Network (AAHN): http://www.aahnet.org
>
> Founded by Meka Hunt and Akosua Magee in 2002, this organization seeks to connect families with educational resources and information. The site supports a chat room, an electronic discussion list, and a pen pal network for children.
>
> African-American Unschooling: http://www.afamunschool.com
>
> This site includes general information and information on Afrocentric resources and offers free subscriptions to the electronic magazine *Fungasa*.
>
> National African-American Homeschoolers Alliance (NAAHA): http://www.naaha.com
>
> This organization was founded by a homeschooling family who sought to bring together African American homeschoolers throughout the country and offer them support. The site includes support group information, articles, and a blog. Free membership includes a subscription to the bimonthly magazine *Homeschooling Matters*.
>
> National Black Home Educators (NBHE): http://www.nbhe.net
>
> This networking organization was founded by a homeschooling couple in 2000. The website offers information, and the organization supports a newsletter and annual conference.

military homeschoolers, who are generally required to follow the laws of the state or country in which they reside, even if they're living overseas.

Libraries near military bases are those most likely to encounter military homeschoolers. Serving them is essentially no different from serving other homeschoolers, although these libraries would be kind to provide ready access to legal information about homeschooling throughout the fifty states and internationally. Librarians should also be aware of Valerie Bonham Moon's website, The Military Homeschooler (www.militaryhomeschoolers.com), a comprehensive resource that addresses a full range of homeschooling issues along with a focus on issues of particular interest to military homeschoolers.

ARTISTS AS HOMESCHOOLERS

People with careers in the arts (writers, musicians, actors, film crew members, etc.) encounter a particular set of challenges when they have children. They often have to keep irregular schedules, making it difficult for families to balance time together and a regimented schoolday. Some artists work at home. Others travel a great deal. Children who are actors face a host of practical issues when trying to balance work and an education. For some families, homeschooling is an enticing option that solves such practical issues. Take as an example the Walton family profiled in a recent issue of *Kiplinger's Personal Finance Magazine:* the mother is a violinist who does soundtrack and studio work, the father is a member of the Los Angeles Police Department, and their two homeschooled sons pursue a variety of interests, including, in the case of the younger, acting jobs and playing Scrabble in French.[2] Families like these often have some kind of philosophical inclination, but homeschooling can also be a practical way for them to preserve family time, ensure the family's professional needs are being met, and provide children with high-quality educations.

ECLECTIC HOMESCHOOLERS

Eclectic homeschoolers make it their business to explore the world of homeschooling to find the methods that work best for their families. These homeschoolers tend to be pragmatists who look at things like children's learning styles, cost, and time investment when thinking about where to take their homeschooling next. Many eclectic homeschoolers favor unit studies and work to build on children's strengths, weaknesses, and interests. To be sure, almost all homeschoolers are eclectic to some degree, but an increasing number of homeschoolers see this as their primary identity. Some of these people might have called themselves unschoolers ten years ago, but the increase in the number and profile of what are often called "radical unschoolers" have made some people uncomfortable with the term.

RESOURCES

Websites of Interest to Military Homeschoolers

Alternative Military Family Electronic Discussion List: http://groups.yahoo.com/group/alternativemilitaryfamily/

This active list is for military families who have chosen to live alternative lifestyles, including but not limited to homeschooling.

Department of Defense Education Activity (DoDEA): http://www.dodea.edu

The DoDEA operates schools nationally and internationally to serve the children of military service members and Department of Defense civilian employees.

Home School Legal Defense Association (HSLDA): http://www.hslda.org

HSLDA maintains information on homeschooling laws for all fifty states as well as U.S. territories.

Homeschooling in the Military Electronic Discussion List: http://groups.yahoo.com/group/homeschoolinginthemilitary/

This inclusive discussion list is for all military homeschoolers.

Military Homeschool Electronic Discussion List: http://groups.yahoo.com/group/military-homeschool/

This active discussion list is for Christian military homeschoolers.

The Military Homeschooler: http://www.militaryhomeschoolers.com

Former homeschooler Valerie Bonham Moon maintains links to pertinent documents from the Department of Defense and other government agencies as well as links to information about national and international support groups for military homeschoolers.

National Home Education Network (NHEN): http://www.nhen.org/leginfo/state_list.asp

NHEN maintains information on homeschooling laws for all fifty states as well as U.S. territories.

> **PROFILE**

Renae Meyer

Renae Meyer, whose husband serves as master chief yeoman in the U.S. Coast Guard at their headquarters in Washington, DC, has been homeschooling for nine years through four duty stations. When their oldest child was old enough to start kindergarten, Meyer and her husband weren't happy with the public schools where they were living, and they couldn't afford a private school. Then a friend took Meyer to a homeschooling seminar. "My husband and I prayed about it and felt that God was calling us to homeschool our kids. We only had two then, one about to start school, and now with four, three in school, the calling is even stronger. We are certain His word has appointed us to raise them up in the ways of the Lord and to point them to Jesus through everything they study."

Now that they are actively homeschooling three of their four children, the Meyers have opted for a curriculum that focuses all of the children on the same topic while allowing each to complete work appropriate to his or her individual level. One of the particular advantages of homeschooling for a military family, Meyer says, is that it is "one of the constants in lives that are disrupted regularly." One of their biggest challenges through their moves has been figuring out each state's homeschooling laws, but Meyer reports that the HSLDA has been a help. She has found only a few military homeschoolers at each station, although "someone who has been living there a while will direct the new ones to the support groups, curriculum sales, and help with legal info."

The Meyers' oldest is "a true bookworm," and the family has been known to visit the library at a new station even before getting their boxes unpacked. Libraries are a vital part of their homeschooling, and through their moves they have experienced a variety of libraries and policies, some of which have been more helpful than others. Loan periods and item limits have been concerns in some libraries: "If the check-out times are two weeks or less, that means more trips and less time to dive into the books." Meyer points out that, with the large number of materials the family borrows, even returning them one day late can result in a hefty fine. "I would love to see us acknowledged as teachers at the library so we don't have late fees or due dates on the books we use. We were in one system that did that for public school teachers but wouldn't do it for homeschoolers." The Meyer family's homeschooling budget isn't large, and at times interlibrary loan costs have proved to be prohibitive enough to limit their access to materials.

Meyer recommends that librarians who want to support homeschoolers consider simple steps such as creating display space for homeschoolers' work, making meeting rooms available at no cost to homeschooling groups, encouraging homeschooled teens to volunteer, having a bulletin board where local homeschooling groups can post information, and, especially for families who move frequently, being flexible about the types of identification needed to obtain a library card. She reports: "The library system we are a part of now is the first we have been in that recognizes homeschoolers. The first time we went and filled our 'box,' they asked if we homeschool. They have a free interlibrary loan program. It is easy to renew online and search the catalog online. There is a max per card as opposed to per family, so we can check out up to 150 books. They notify you by e-mail when your books are due. Now if they would just drop or cap the late fees, it would be almost perfect."

NOTES

1. Daniel Princiotta and Stacey Bielick, *Homeschooling in the United States: 2003* (Washington, DC: National Center for Education Statistics, 2005), 9. Available online at http://nces.ed.gov/pubs2006/homeschool/.
2. "Fun and Learning," *Kiplinger's Personal Finance Magazine*, August 2006, 24.

PART II
SERVING HOMESCHOOLERS

Connecting with Homeschoolers in Your Community

The key to developing successful programs and services for homeschoolers is to figure out who the homeschoolers in your community are and how to reach them. There are almost certainly existing support groups, electronic discussion lists, newsletters, and other lines of communication in your area, and discovering how to tap into them gives you excellent opportunities to solicit information, get feedback, and target your marketing most effectively. It also allows you to talk to some of the homeschoolers in your community, which is the best way to begin to learn which niches of the homeschooling world are most prevalent in your area.

WHERE DO I START?

If you have no clue who the homeschoolers are in your community, the simplest—but perhaps most daunting—way to connect with them is to start noticing when they visit the library and find a way to strike up a conversation. You are probably seeing homeschoolers without really *seeing* them, so start paying attention. Families with school-age kids in the library during school hours can be a dead giveaway, although tread lightly since there are any number of other legitimate reasons parents might be in the library with their school-age children in the middle of the day. Parents and children asking for large amounts of materials on a particular topic can be a clue, as can families who regularly troop in with backpacks, tote bags, or rolling carts to take materials home. These families are often familiar faces, people who visit the library once a week or more.

When you think you've identified a homeschooling family, work up a little nerve and find a way to ask a parent if they are, indeed, homeschooling. This can be a natural part of a standard reference interview. Knowing what a person intends to use materials for gives you a better idea how to direct that person, and you might send a parent who is building a unit study to different resources than you would a parent who is simply looking for a little casual reading material. If the parent chooses to identify himself or herself as a homeschooler, saying something positive along the lines of "That's great. We've been thinking of trying to build up a homeschooling collection for the library" might get the homeschooler talking. If you manage to develop a rapport, you can start asking questions: Why did you decide to homeschool? Are you using a curriculum? What kinds of materials are you using? Are you part of any local groups? Are you interested in suggesting some materials for our collection? It's sort of obvious, but showing interest goes a long way toward building trust and a positive feeling about the library. Homeschoolers encounter a lot of people who question what they're doing and why they're doing it. They can be reluctant to open up to people who don't seem enthusiastic and interested. Once they've decided that someone is, indeed, genuinely interested, they are almost always helpful.

IDENTIFYING LOCAL ORGANIZATIONS AND SUPPORT GROUPS

You may have trouble identifying, approaching, or obtaining information from the homeschoolers who visit your library. Even if you find homeschoolers who are willing to talk, if they aren't movers and shakers in your local homeschooling community they may not know about all of the organizations and support groups in your area. It pays to put some time into identifying local organizations, support groups, and those who run them.

This is a task much easier said than done. Homeschoolers are always evolving. Just for starters, kids aren't kids forever. Homeschoolers who are extremely involved in local networks may drop out entirely when their children move on. They may get busy. They may decide to spend a long period of time traveling. They may have a new baby. There are all kinds of reasons parents who are active in the local homeschooling scene one year are not so the next. This leads to evolving leadership, groups that change mission and function, groups or newsletters that suddenly stop operating, and a general mess if you're trying to find groups active in your area.

The Internet is a good place to start. Librarians may be surprised at what an old-fashioned Google search can turn up. Try searching the name of your city, town, or county along with the word "homeschool," and see what happens. You might uncover a local homeschooler's blog or an electronic discussion list or the home pages of local support groups. All of these can be rich sources of information. If that doesn't pan out, a few websites maintain listings of local support groups. Again, because of the evolving nature of the homeschooling world, lists like these can only be so current. Still, the even more rapidly evolving Internet makes it one of the more likely places to find something useful and current.

Several websites maintain fairly reliable listings of homeschooling groups, but two are especially useful. HUUmans on the Web (www.uuhomeschool.org) is geared toward Unitarian Universalist homeschoolers and, in keeping with that group's policy, toward "kindred spirits." The site maintains a listing of groups that are 100 percent inclusive—anyone can join. The groups in this listing tend to be eclectic, and their strengths lie in sharing information. For example, under "New York State," HUUmans on the Web lists Simply Homeschooling (http://groups.yahoo.com/group/simplyhomeschooling/), an electronic discussion list for homeschoolers in the greater Rochester area. In a county serving just over 1,600 homeschoolers, Simply Homeschooling has 255 subscribers and averages two or three messages a day. Only homeschoolers can join the list, but the list owner is happy to post library information when she receives it. Postings to this list almost always generate a response.

The Home School Legal Defense Organization (www.hslda.org) also maintains a listing of state and local homeschooling organizations, although like HSLDA itself the listing tends to focus on organizations that have a conservative Protestant bent or are exclusively for conservative Protestants. Many of these organizations require families who join to sign a statement of faith, and some have dress codes and other requirements for group functions. The CenLa Christian Homeschool Association of Louisiana (www.cchsa.net) is a good example. Families who join are required to sign a statement that indicates that they agree with certain Christian doctrinal statements. No one can nail down the statistics with any accuracy, but there is no doubt that there are a large number of conservative Protestant homeschoolers in the United States. Almost every public library has at least some conservative Protestant homeschoolers in its community, and the conservative Protestant networks tend to be strong and well organized. If you want to reach out to homeschoolers, this is a segment of the population you cannot afford to ignore.

OTHER ORGANIZATIONS AND BUSINESSES THAT CATER TO HOMESCHOOLERS

It goes without saying that homeschoolers don't exist in a vacuum. Public libraries are the community organizations most likely to attract large numbers of homeschoolers, but there are others. Many YMCAs, for example, offer special sports and fitness programs for homeschoolers. In some areas, homeschoolers have formed their own scouting troops. 4-H clubs also tend to attract homeschoolers. Leaders in these organizations may be able to put you in touch with the homeschoolers they work with or to disseminate information you provide.

Local churches are another excellent place to connect with homeschoolers. Most libraries and librarians don't do cooperative work with churches, but there is no reason not to. Why not talk to the pastors and ministers of local churches? If they are serving significant numbers of homeschoolers, they are likely to know about it, and if you are trying to get the word out about services that will help those homeschoolers, they may be willing to post fliers, make brochures available, or run press releases in church bulletins. Some may even make your events part of their weekly announcements during services. Although this might require you to step a little out of your comfort zone, and you could encounter people who aren't interested in helping you, making a good connection could be a positive step for libraries and the community.

In addition to nonprofit entities, plenty of local businesses cater to the homeschooling crowd. Libraries could consider posting fliers at local grocery stories, co-ops, natural food stores, craft stores, consignment shops, thrift stores, bookstores, teacher supply stores, and toy stores. This isn't necessarily the best way to reach families, but it is good to get information out there in as many ways as possible when you're starting out.

PROFILE

Rochester Area Homeschoolers Association

Sue Klassen, a homeschooling mother of eleven years who, along with her daughter, coedits the Rochester (New York) Area Homeschoolers Association's (RAHA) monthly newsletter, reports that the RAHA mission is to be "a community of families dedicated to supporting one another in our common commitment to learning without schooling. Our membership gathers together for philosophical rather than religious reasons and therefore welcomes families of all backgrounds who share our vision. We are deeply devoted to our children and believe that their growth is best fostered in a child-led, rather than curriculum-driven, learning environment that is centered in the home and reaches out to explore the world around us." Membership is open to any homeschooler who shares RAHA's vision, and a small annual membership fee covers the cost of necessities such as meeting room space and newsletter distribution. RAHA's board organizes monthly meetings and other basic functions, but the group as a whole focuses on activities and initiatives organized by its membership. RAHA provides members with a phone list, and members can elect to participate in an e-mail list. "Members are encouraged to reach out to each other using these tools, and to organize events and invite others," says Klassen. "And RAHA members do. RAHA members are constantly connecting in book groups and on warm afternoons in parks, in chess clubs and on the ski slopes, in drama groups and on camping trips." RAHA also maintains a website (www.rochesterareahomeschoolers.org).

Klassen's family joined two groups when they started homeschooling, but they found that they began building strong friendships through RAHA. "RAHA provided not only peer support but the space for deep friendships to grow." The family participated in many regular and spontaneous activities with fellow members, and today, Klassen reports, "though some of our children are now in college, these bonds remain strong—we still gather together for events and just to be together." Through their work on RAHA's newsletter, Klassen's

> daughter has learned that she enjoys designing newsletters and then, by extension, websites. At sixteen, she's done newsletters and Web work for other organizations and is considering a career in graphic design. "I can't imagine homeschooling without RAHA," says Sue Klassen.

CONFERENCES AND CURRICULUM FAIRS

One of the most interesting ways to make connections with homeschoolers and the homeschooling world is by attending local homeschooling conferences, workshops, or curriculum fairs. Some events might not allow non-homeschoolers to attend, but if you take the time to contact the organizers they may make an exception. Attending an event where homeschooling vendors display and sell their products gives librarians an opportunity to examine a variety of curriculums, products, services, and organizations. You can get your hands on materials and talk to people who know the products best. Some things you see may not be appropriate for library collections for one reason or another—because they're too expensive, for instance, or not durably constructed. Still, you are almost certainly going to find things that could be useful, often things that haven't been reviewed at all in library publications. If you attend a local event, you're likely to run into homeschoolers who frequent your library. They will be impressed by your interest in being there, and this will give you a valuable opportunity to network outside the library.

Workshops and presentations at conferences can be similarly enlightening. Some of them are more directly applicable to library work than others, but all provide valuable insights into some of the ways homeschoolers operate. What are their concerns? How do they do what they do? Again, the opportunity to network, talk to people, and be seen is instructive for you and helps homeschoolers realize that the library is serious about serving their needs.

SURVEYS AND FOCUS GROUPS

As you begin to identify your homeschoolers and the best ways to connect with them, you are probably going to be gathering a lot of informal data through conversation and observation. You will start to learn what some families are looking for and what kind of philosophies they subscribe to. One or even a few families' thoughts and experiences are probably not a good guide for the thoughts and feelings of the homeschooling community as a whole. As we established in part 1 of this book, homeschoolers are an extremely diverse population. Librarians need to be careful not to make assumptions and generalizations, and they should try to avoid catering to the dominant or most vocal groups. If your community has a large number of fundamentalist Protestant homeschoolers, for instance, you should make a point of serving them, but it is important to maintain balance by providing attention and services to other homeschoolers as well.

Libraries serving the smallest communities should probably think twice about doing surveys: they aren't likely to get more out of a survey than they would out of causal conversations with homeschoolers they know. Smaller and mid-size libraries might consider pooling resources to survey a larger area—a county instead of a town, for instance. Larger library systems can net the largest samples and gather the most statistically significant data, but, of course, when you survey a wide area you lose the benefit of local information. Working with professional researchers is the best way to design a nonbiased survey, but many libraries don't have funds to devote to surveying the smaller local population.

All this said, surveys and focus groups can be extremely instructive when you are trying to assess your homeschooling community and its needs. You can look to the bibliography's program development listings for the finer points of designing and running surveys—but the following are a few simple suggestions and cautions.

If you ever have the inclination or opportunity to explore the available research on homeschooling, you will quickly learn that the usefulness of many studies is limited by the extreme difficulty of getting representative, nonbiased samples of homeschoolers—because there are, in the grand scheme of things, so few of them. And then there are the typical survey pitfalls. If you do an in-house pencil-and-paper survey of homeschoolers, for instance, you hear only from the homeschoolers who are already using the library. If you send a survey to the local unschooling electronic discussion list, you get only the unschoolers' perspectives. If you post a survey on your website, you get only the computer-savvy homeschoolers who frequent your site.

If you decide to survey your homeschooling population, spend some time thinking about the segmentation of your community and how to best assess various segments' needs. Local organizations are the logical places to start. Most areas with a homeschooling community of any size very likely have at least one secular/inclusive organization as well as a conservative Protestant organization; many communities have more. Organizations obviously have some overlap in terms of membership and needs, but it can be helpful to survey each group and then compile and analyze the results separately. This allows your library to see the similarities and differences between groups and may provide some insights into how to best work with each. Perhaps the surveys will show that homeschoolers are dissatisfied across the board with the library's borrowing period, that the members of the secular group are generally satisfied with the library's collection, but that the conservative Protestant group can't find materials they need when they visit the library. This information might lead the library to revisit borrowing rules and perhaps conduct a focus group with members of the Protestant organization to inquire about what types of materials they're looking for and not finding, which in turn could lead to an education/marketing effort or a project to strengthen part of the collection.

What you do not want to do when looking at surveys is jump to conclusions and take action too hastily. Keep your sample size in mind. If you are surveying only ten people, the results can be interesting, but they aren't going to be terribly significant unless nine or ten of those people say the same thing. The concerns of one or two people can sometimes be indicative of others' concerns or can reveal holes in collections and services to minorities, but sometimes they are just one person's individual issue.

Some issues have a reasonable and practical solution, and others don't. If homeschoolers are overwhelmingly dissatisfied with loan periods, for example, it may very well be that other heavy borrowers are also dissatisfied, making this an issue well worth considering. If homeschoolers overwhelmingly want their small library to invest in expensive curriculum packages, though (some cost hundreds of dollars), it may simply not be feasible. When deciding how to respond to survey data, it pays to gather as much data as you can, ask a lot of questions, and spend some time carefully considering cost versus benefit, how changes might impact other library users, and what options promise the greatest positive impact. For an excellent example of how libraries can gather information about their homeschooling population, see Amy McCarthy and Deborah Lines Andersen's *JLAMS* study "Homeschoolers at the Public Library: Are Library Services and Policies Keeping Pace?"[1] Or consider the basic e-mail survey in the following box.

"Serving Homeschoolers" E-mail Survey

1. How often does your family use the library?[2]
   - more than once a week
   - weekly
   - more than once a month
   - monthly
   - other

2. What resources does your family use or search for at the library? (Choose all that apply.)
   - nonfiction
   - fiction
   - videos (DVD or VHS)
   - music
   - audiobooks
   - computer software
   - reference books
   - Internet access
   - homeschooling how-to
   - library programs (including storytimes)

3. How often does your family use the library's online resources (website, library catalog, online databases, etc.)?
   - never
   - weekly
   - more than once a month
   - monthly
   - other

4. Does your family use the online catalog from your home computer?
   - yes
   - no

5. When you visit the library, do you usually find materials by yourself or ask a librarian for assistance?
   - by myself
   - ask for assistance
   - both

6. How well does your local library (staff, available materials, programs, etc.) meet your needs as a homeschooling family?
   - exceeds our needs
   - adequately meets our needs
   - often fails to meet our needs
   - never meets our needs

7. What would you most like to see added to the library's collection or programs to better serve you as a homeschooling family?

PROFILE

Melissa Painton

For two years, librarian Melissa Painton served as the coordinator of the "Serving Homeschoolers" Parent and Child Services Grant awarded by the New York State Library to four Monroe County libraries. When she started, one of Painton's first tasks was to establish a grant advisory board of parents representing local homeschooling groups. When she started out, she was aware of several groups active in Monroe County, including Loving Education at Home (LEAH), Rochester Area Homeschoolers Association (RAHA), and the Simply Homeschooling electronic discussion list (http://groups.yahoo.com/group/simplyhomeschooling/). She also knew of at least one Catholic homeschooling group. Reaching representatives of these groups turned out to be more complicated than Painton first suspected.

Representatives of the local LEAH group and RAHA were involved in the grant process from its inception, so making contact with them was relatively easy. Painton became aware of the Simply Homeschooling electronic discussion list only when she started working on the grant and began subscribing to lists in an effort to learn more about homeschooling. Simply Homeschooling was local, which made it of particular interest, but because of concerns about confidentiality its subscription was moderated and open only to homeschoolers. In her attempt to subscribe, Painton started e-mailing with the list's moderator, who, it turned out, was happy to share library information with the list and also willing to serve on the grant's advisory board.

The Catholic homeschooling group proved slightly more difficult to find because it didn't seem to have a website and Painton couldn't find anything about who was running the group. Finally, though, she learned that the group had recently changed its name from Catholic Homeschoolers of Western New York to St. Thomas Aquinas Homeschoolers of the Rochester Area, and she finally got an e-mail address she believed was current. After several weeks of attempts, she made contact and learned that someone already on the advisory board was a member of the group and willing to pass along information about library programs and services.

> Overall, Painton reports, the effort was worthwhile: "The advisory board was an effective means of disseminating grant information through the various networks of homeschoolers." Surveys showed that the majority of people who attended the libraries' homeschooling programs heard about them through information passed on by advisory board members, confirming the idea that announcements passed along by fellow homeschoolers would hold more weight than those coming directly from library staff. Painton used these networks to disseminate information as well as to solicit information in the form of surveys and recommendations.

TRADITIONAL MARKETING

Targeted marketing is the best way to reach any audience, but the traditional marketing methods most libraries fall back on may prove effective with homeschoolers as well. Press releases and ads in local newspapers, blurbs on the library's website, library signage, and take-home fliers are the basic ways most libraries get the word out about their programs. In larger libraries, make sure that programs for homeschoolers appear in fliers for all age levels concerned—children, teens, and adults. Also consider creating a special area in the library to post announcements for homeschoolers. A designated bulletin board or even a shelf or two of space gives staff and homeschoolers a place where they know they can find the latest information on programs and services.

HOMESCHOOLERS AS VOLUNTEERS

Many prominent writers and thinkers in the homeschooling movement have talked about the importance of "real work" in the education of children. John Holt asserted that one reason institutional schools don't truly reach children is that so much schoolwork is meaningless beyond completing a particular task and getting a grade. Raymond and Dorothy Moore shared this assessment and further stressed the importance of service to the community in the development of character. Volunteering is a cornerstone of many families' homeschooling routines. Like other volunteers, homeschoolers welcome opportunities to do meaningful work, explore interests, build skills, strengthen connections to the community, and give back to organizations that are important to them. Since so many homeschoolers are among libraries' most avid users, working with them as volunteers can be a particularly excellent fit for all concerned.

Homeschoolers can make unusual, valuable contributions to any library's volunteer program. At the most basic, homeschooled children and teens may be available to volunteer during school hours when institutionally schooled children cannot. Homeschooled families may also be willing—even eager—to volunteer as a group. It is amazing how quickly tedious tasks can be completed—preparing a mailing, for instance, or producing program brochures—with a parent and a few eager children on the job. As a bonus, reaching out to and working with homeschooled volunteers is another way to build a relationship with the homeschooling community at large. The library learns more about homeschoolers while homeschoolers learn more about the library. This kind of exchange can promote positive feelings, the flow of information, and the word-of-mouth advertising that helps libraries and library programs thrive. These are benefits of working with volunteers in general, of course, but the benefits become even more important when the library is trying to reach an underserved population.

Setting up a volunteer program from scratch is beyond the scope of this book, but the bibliography includes resources for libraries interested in starting or expanding a volunteer program, including Kellie M. Gillespie's excellent *Teen Volunteer Services in Libraries*. Libraries that already have established programs can easily incorporate homeschoolers with a little advertising push: send multiple copies of volunteer applications to local homeschooling groups, attend local homeschool group meetings to talk about volunteer opportunities at the library, or send an e-mail to local homeschooling e-mail lists. Make sure your volunteer application leaves some way for homeschoolers to identify themselves and their availability. Websites, community bulletin boards, and even in-library signage can be other ways to pull in a surprising number of volunteers.

TEEN ADVISORY BOARDS

One of the biggest trends in teen services over the past decade has been the growth of teen advisory boards—teens who serve as volunteers and provide guidance on library services to other teens. Most librarians encourage their teen boards to do meaningful work, such as selecting materials for the library's collection, planning and implementing programs, providing input into teen spaces, advertising library programs, providing content for

PROFILE

Marcia Weinert

Marcia Weinert's homeschooling journey began when her family moved from Mississippi to New York. As president-elect of the PTA in their school district in Mississippi, Weinert's pet project had been building a successful and active parent volunteer program. In New York, she had a hard time getting anyone in the local district to allow her to volunteer at all. What became even more frustrating was that her bright and academically successful son began having an increasingly difficult time emotionally dealing with the school's expectations of what he could and should be doing. In Mississippi, Weinert had begun seriously exploring the literature on parental involvement in education, and as she spent more time in schools she started to suspect that institutional schools might not be the best way to educate children at all. "Motherhood," she concluded, "is the best model for teaching, and not the other way around." After half a year in the new district, she pulled her three children (one kindergartener, one first grader, and one fourth grader) out of school and began unschooling.

With her history in volunteering, it's no wonder that one of Weinert's first thoughts was to encourage her children to volunteer. When she asked what they wanted to do, they all agreed that they wanted to work at the humane society, but because of liability issues the humane society would not let children interact directly with animals. Being avid readers and library users, one of the next places they looked was the local public library, where they wound up stamping date due cards on a regular basis. Even Weinert's youngest had the manual dexterity to stamp a date due card, and all her children thoroughly enjoyed working with stamps and stickers. They felt like they were making a difference. "Most people want to be helpful," says Weinert, "even young children."

After a while, the family was promoted to replacing the spine labels on books in the mystery collection and, as the years went by, they all got involved in other library volunteer projects, such as assisting with children's programs, setting up for the Friends of the Library annual book sale, and serving on the library's Teen Advisory Board. All three children also became paid members of the library

> staff in their teen years. When asked what her children gained from their volunteer experiences, Weinert replies that they quickly became confident and comfortable library users who were happy to seek out information, including staff assistance, without adult intervention. They had a feeling of ownership and independence that continues to serve them well.
>
> Now that all of her children are in college, Marcia Weinert has become a full-fledged library assistant, so the irony is that she currently gets paid to work with volunteers in the same library where she and her children began volunteering so many years before. She sees welcoming homeschoolers as volunteers as a win-win situation for homeschoolers and for libraries: "Many homeschoolers look for opportunities to volunteer, and homeschoolers are an underserved population. This is another place to invite them into the building and get acquainted with them and their needs and interests." Weinert also points to the large number of homeschoolers she knows who served as volunteers as children or teens and have grown up to become paid employees, even going so far as to become librarians themselves. These are the kinds of benefits that last a lifetime.

newsletters and websites, and advertising library programs and services in myriad ways. Homeschoolers can make excellent additions to teen advisory boards. As is the case with homeschoolers volunteering in any capacity, they can provide a rare perspective, help librarians learn more about what homeschoolers are looking for, and bring the library's message to other homeschoolers. Again, it's often just a matter of libraries remembering to let the homeschoolers know they're welcome.

ADVOCACY

Whether or not it comes naturally to them, most homeschooling parents find themselves in positions in which they must learn to promote their children's best interests. Consequently, homeschoolers can be more likely than the average person on the street to support other things they think are important—the library, for instance. A few studies have suggested that homeschoolers are more active in the community than the average citizen. One found that 76 percent of homeschooled adults (as opposed to 29 percent of adults as a whole) voted within a specified five-year period.[3] Homeschoolers are the kind of people who can often be counted on to write letters, march in rallies, and bring problems to the attention of others in the community.

Once libraries have built relationships with homeschoolers, they should make a point of sharing information about budget votes, potential threats, new initiatives, and other issues that may affect (positively or negatively) library services that homeschoolers rely on. Many homeschoolers, even children, are happy to contribute in small and large ways to efforts to support and enhance an institution they use and enjoy.

NOTES

1. Amy McCarthy and Deborah Lines Andersen, "Homeschoolers at the Public Library: Are Library Services and Policies Keeping Pace?" *JLAMS* 3, no. 1 (2006–2007), http://www.nyla.org/content/user_10/JLAMSspring07wg.pdf.
2. This survey, which gathered data from three homeschooling organizations in Monroe County, New York, was made possible by a New York State 2005–2007 Parent and Child Services Grant from the New York State Library, New York State Education Department.
3. Brian D. Ray, "Homeschoolers on to College: What Research Shows Us," *Journal of College Admission*, Fall 2004, 5–11.

8

Creating Programs with Homeschoolers in Mind

One of the most important basic programs a library can offer homeschoolers is that which teaches children, teens, and even parents how to better utilize the library, its resources, and information in general. Library skills are part of many statewide curriculums and educational standards, and in some states homeschoolers are required to cover library skills as part of their homeschooling program. A little research into your state's homeschooling laws should tell you whether this is the case in your state.

Even if your state doesn't require library skills instruction, homeschoolers tend to be extremely heavy library users and may be eager to learn more about how they can get the most of out the library and its resources. Being experts on information and how to use it, librarians are the ideal people to develop and run these programs—akin, in many parents' eyes, to taking their child to a musician to learn how to play the piano. Libraries can use these programs as vehicles to build stronger relationships with the homeschooling community while helping homeschoolers become more confident and independent library users.

These days, few public libraries are offering library skills classes to the general public, and if they are they often cover only basic topics, which leaves most librarians who want to offer such programs to homeschoolers at a bit of a loss. The first step in developing any program is to gather information. Chapter 7 offers several techniques librarians can use to determine what their homeschooling population is interested in.

Different communities have approached library skills instruction to homeschoolers in a variety of ways with much success. Some opt for something as basic as an annual orientation much like the type of tour one might offer a scouting troop or other community organization. More ambitious libraries have built a series of programs that focus on topics such as the difference between fiction and nonfiction, how to use the Dewey Decimal System, and how to use the library catalog. More involved information literacy programs might delve into such topics as the parts of a book, types of reference sources, and evaluating Internet resources. Some libraries even offer classes on using computer applications to report the results of one's research—using desktop publishing software to create a brochure, for instance, or creating a web page from scratch. Depending on the size of the community, available resources, and librarians' and homeschoolers' levels of mutual interest, there is a broad spectrum of possibilities.

A NOTE ABOUT AGE LEVELS

Almost all youth services librarians wrestle with questions surrounding age levels when planning programs. Programmers have to balance what they want to accomplish with the composition and needs of the community in order to create a program that is valuable, enjoyed, and attended by enough people to make the effort worthwhile. These questions become even more interesting when one is talking about homeschoolers. Homeschoolers are a growing population, but they are still only a small percentage of the community as a whole, which makes for a smaller pool of people to draw from. Statistics suggest that homeschoolers tend to have larger families than the general population, and parents with more than one child are generally more inclined to make an effort to attend programs that more than one of their children can attend. These factors lead many librarians to create programs for wider age spans, but there's something to be said for programs targeted to narrow age and ability levels. Then again, since homeschoolers operate outside typical school frameworks, the abilities and interests of homeschooled children may not correlate with what one expects of institutionally schooled children of the same age anyway.

The best thing to do is talk to homeschoolers and work collaboratively to design something workable and appealing. Cathy Henderson of the Greece Public Library (New York), whose programs are profiled later in this chapter, solved the age level dilemma by running two hour-long programs back to back—one for children in grades K–2 followed by one for children in grades 3–5. At the Bethel Park Public Library (Pennsylvania), the librarians realized that some families were driving a substantial distance to attend their programs, so they offered 2½-hour sessions for wider age spans (grades 1–5 or grades 6 and up) during the lunch hour and invited participants to bring a bag lunch. At the Webster Public Library (New York), we have offered library skills classes to homeschooling parents in our computer lab in conjunction with a supervised activity for children in our children's programming room; as a bonus, the activities for children have been run by homeschooled teens. The point is not to create the perfect program that serves everyone's needs but to create—with some information, flexibility, and creativity—high-quality programs that serve a large portion of your homeschooling population well.

TYPES OF PROGRAMS

Orientations

At the most basic, libraries can develop an annual orientation program for homeschoolers. This program might be an hour or ninety minutes and would include a tour of the library along with an overview of resources and services of particular interest to homeschoolers. This would not have to be all that different from what the library offers any community group that requests a tour. Librarians can gear the orientation toward children, teens, or parents—or they can welcome families to attend the program together. Orientations are relatively easy for most libraries to put together. Still, they let homeschoolers know they are welcome in the library, they give librarians an opportunity to interact directly with homeschoolers, and they can be a valuable marketing tool. They can be a way for smaller libraries to create a meaningful program for homeschoolers and for larger libraries to begin developing a relationship with the homeschooling community.

Basic Library Skills

Libraries may also offer basic library skills classes. Such classes would likely be age-targeted and teach the skills that help individuals navigate the library. Topics typically covered include fiction classification, the Dewey Decimal System, and the library catalog. Most of these topics are best suited to an older audience or at least an audience that can read. It is also

> **RESOURCES**
>
> ## Games for Library Instruction
>
> Lee, Carol K., and Fay Edwards. *57 Games to Play in the Library or Classroom.* Fort Atkinson, WI: Alleyside Press, 1997.
>
> Lee, Carol K., and Janet Langford. *Learning about Books and Libraries: A Gold Mine of Games.* Fort Atkinson, WI: Alleyside Press, 2000.
>
> Lee, Carol K., and Janet Langford. *Learning about Books and Libraries 2.* Fort Atkinson, WI: UpstartBooks, 2003.
>
> Miller, Pat. *Stretchy Library Lessons: Library Skills.* Fort Atkinson, WI: UpstartBooks, 2003.

possible to design programs in which children and teens work together to learn through collaborative problem solving. Participants from larger families are probably already used to working this way, since families often engage in cooperative learning activities that span age groups as part of their daily routines. Library skills classes normally run an hour to an hour and a half and should focus on one or two topics at most. Many books exist to help librarians design classes, games, and activities that teach library skills; for more information, see the "Games for Library Instruction" box and the bibliography.

More Advanced Information Literacy Skills

Libraries may take library skills a step further and design in-depth information literacy programs. These could include topics such as the parts of a book, fiction versus nonfiction, using reference sources, evaluating websites, and using various style guides to cite sources. These types of classes might be offered in response to a specific need or demand or as part of an ongoing weekly, monthly, or otherwise regular series. Librarians have an easier time reaching children and teens and building more advanced skills through regular sessions in which everyone can develop a comfort level, ask questions, practice skills, and build knowledge in stages. *Information Power: Building Partnerships for Learning*, from AASL and AECT, is one of the most useful books for those thinking about building more advanced information literacy programs, and *Teaching Library Media Skills in*

PROFILE

Cathy Henderson

When children's librarian Cathy Henderson started working at the Seymour Library in Brockport, New York, she began noticing that homeschooling patrons seemed nervous. Sensing that they were reluctant to approach her, Henderson began to approach them. That's when she learned that a previous library employee had told homeschoolers that they were taking up too much time and room and couldn't "hang out" at the library anymore. Henderson was horrified, but this began a dialog between her and some homeschooling parents who, it turned out, were receptive and had a lot to say. With their input, she began putting together a series of library skills programs designed especially for homeschoolers.

The homeschoolers Henderson was talking to reported doing school-type work in the mornings, so she planned monthly programs in the afternoon in a two-hour back-to-back time slot: one program for kids in grades K–2, one for grades 3–5. She advertised the topics—starting with basics like the Dewey Decimal System and fiction versus nonfiction—and gave parents the flexibility to determine which group would be the best fit for their children. "The parents know their children best," says Henderson. In a community of fewer than 20,000 people, Henderson soon had a loyal group of about thirty homeschooled children attending her library skills classes. She believes that timing, age flexibility, and consecutive time slots accommodated a wide range of families' needs and were instrumental in the programs' success. She was pleased to see that parents took advantage of the time in which their children were otherwise occupied to socialize and share information. Henderson encountered a variety of homeschoolers in Brockport, but that didn't seem to impact her programs. "I didn't ask them about their philosophy. I wanted them to know that, no matter why they were homeschooling, I was here to help them."

The homeschooling community in Brockport was heartbroken when Henderson left to begin a new job as head of the children's department at the Greece Public Library in Greece, New York. Greece serves a much larger population of 94,000 people, and Henderson made building services to homeschoolers a priority in her new position.

> She's been running her library skills classes essentially the same way she did in Brockport, delving into more advanced research skills, such as how to use reference sources and library databases. Ironically, she finds that fewer children attend her homeschooling programs in a community almost five times the size of that at her old library. She thinks information isn't moving through the homeschooling community in Greece as effectively as it was in Brockport partly because the community is larger and she hasn't been able to develop the same sorts of relationships with parents. In Brockport she spent most of her time in the Children's Room, but that's not the case in Greece.
>
> Cathy Henderson has continued offering library skills classes to homeschoolers in spite of the lower attendance. "I felt I had a skill that made offering that program unique, and I was the expert in that area." She plans to continue to work with homeschoolers by maintaining her heavily used collection of homeschooling materials, including manuals, homeschooling catalogs, and multimedia kits on language arts topics.

Grades K-6: A How-to-Do-It Manual for Librarians, by Carolyn Garner, is a practical resource for designing programs for children in the primary grades.

Programs for Parents

It is worth making a special note that homeschooling parents may be just as—or even more—interested in library instruction as their young children and teens. Homeschooling parents often say that one of the joys of homeschooling is that they are learning right alongside their children. To that end, it's a good idea to welcome parents into any homeschooling program you offer. Once when I was teaching a class on the Dewey Decimal System to upper elementary-age children, several moms were sitting in the back of the room taking notes, and one even raised her hand halfway through to ask if this was the same system the library used to classify the adult nonfiction collection. I'm sure those parents got as much out of the program as the children did, if not more.

Homeschooling parents may also be interested in programs designed specifically for them. Most use the library to develop or supplement curriculums and unit studies, and they may be looking for a range of information on particular topics at any given time. Their information needs are immediate and often complex, and they may welcome programs that teach them skills that eventually save them time and effort. These are people who believe in the importance of lifelong learning and who would probably be using the library even if they weren't homeschooling, which makes them that much more likely to attend programs on library topics. Programs can tackle any of the subjects listed previously, but parents who are more comfortable with library resources may be interested in classes geared specifically toward identifying and locating the types of items they need for their homeschooling programs. For an example of what is possible, see the box "Finding Fiction by Subject."

Finding Fiction by Subject: A Class for Parents

COURSE OUTLINE

This will be a 90-minute class in the library's computer lab. There will be one hour of formal instruction followed by 30 minutes for exploration and questions.

Objectives:
- Participants will learn how to use the library catalog to find fiction for children and teens by subject.
- Participants will learn how to place holds on materials in the library catalog.
- Participants will learn how to use the NoveList database to identify fiction for children and teens by subject.
- Participants will learn how to use print reference sources to identify fiction for children and teens by subject.

Prerequisites:
- Participants need to be familiar with using a mouse, using a keyboard, and using the Internet.
- Participants need to have used the library catalog to perform basic title, author, or subject searches successfully.

OTHER PROGRAMS

Most libraries begin by offering information literacy programs to homeschoolers, but they can certainly offer any program to homeschoolers that they offer to the general public. It should go without saying that librarians must make sure that homeschoolers are aware of the storytimes, book groups, craft programs, and other activities their libraries are already offering, but they may also consider offering some of these programs specifically to homeschoolers. Some homeschoolers prefer to do activities outside the home while other children are in school, and many enjoy opportunities to network with other homeschoolers. Programs for homeschoolers tend to work best in libraries that serve communities with larger homeschool-

---

Scenario:
- During this class, we will use various sources to locate historical fiction set during the Civil War for children and teens.
    I. Library catalog
       a. Demonstrate a keyword search.
          i. Show parts of a catalog record (title, author, number of pages, summary, subject headings).
          ii. Show how to place items on hold.
          iii. Show how to limit to items owned by the branch that are checked in.
       b. Demonstrate a subject search.
       c. Discuss advantages and disadvantages of keyword and subject searching.
    II. NoveList
       a. Demonstrate subject search.
       b. Demonstrate how to limit by age level, reading level, length, etc.
    III. Reference Books
       a. *A to Zoo: Subject Access to Children's Picture Books,* 7th ed., by Carolyn W. Lima and John A. Lima
       b. *Best Books for Children: Preschool through Grade 6,* 8th ed., by Catherine Barr and John T. Gillespie
       c. *Best Books for Middle School and Junior High Readers: Grades 6–9,* by John T. Gillespie and Catherine Barr
       d. *Best Books for High School Readers: Grades 9–12,* by John T. Gillespie and Catherine Barr

ing populations or where the homeschooling population is active and organized. In any case, as we see throughout this book, seeking homeschoolers' ideas and input on logistical issues (timing, frequency, location, age levels, etc.) helps ensure the success of any programs the library might offer.

Open Houses

Hosting an open house for homeschoolers can be an easy way to welcome homeschoolers into the library and give librarians a chance to showcase services and collections of interest. There are any number of ways to set up this type of event. It could be as easy as setting aside an hour or two when the library serves refreshments and gives homeschoolers an opportunity to peruse homeschooling materials, information about local support groups, legal information, and the like. Libraries could embellish this type of program by hiring a storyteller or speaker—perhaps a lawyer could speak on legal issues pertaining to homeschooling or leaders of local homeschooling groups could give short presentations. Open houses can be relatively inexpensive to put together and can be geared toward the whole family, and they can be a valuable marketing opportunity and way for libraries with limited resources to reach out to their homeschooling community.

Literature-Based Programming

Storytimes, storytelling programs, book groups, and other book-themed events can serve as instructional time in states where this is a requirement, expose children and parents to new books and resources, spark new interests, and enhance language arts instruction. These programs tend to be almost as popular with homeschoolers as they are enjoyable opportunities for youth services librarians to share books they love. In some communities, libraries may have more success targeting these types of programs to homeschoolers than they would targeting them to the community at large.

Storytimes and storytelling programs are flexible and relatively easy to plan and run. Librarians can run them as one-shot programs in the library or as a series. They can welcome the whole family, or they can target a particular age range. Librarians can also offer storytimes as an outreach visit to local homeschooling group meetings. The wealth of options makes these types of programs easy to fit into many different types of communities and situations.

Book groups for homeschoolers work well in many libraries. Homeschoolers are often on the lookout for programs and events that allow their

> **PROFILE**
>
> ## *Bethel Park Public Library*
>
> When the librarians at the Bethel Park (Pennsylvania) Public Library realized how many homeschoolers were in the library's service area, they decided to start offering them programs. They did a needs assessment and learned that their homeschoolers were spread out over a wide area and that many families had more than one child. In response to these needs, they developed a regular series of programs for homeschoolers that has proved quite successful. Children's librarian and certified teacher Lynn Hahn currently offers four programs for homeschoolers each month from September through April: two for grades 1–5 and two for grades 6 and up. Each program focuses on a particular subject (recent topics include ancient Egypt, folklore, and history mysteries) and lasts two and a half hours. Hahn asks homeschoolers to bring a bag lunch and drink, so the children and teens enjoy activity time, a meal, and then more activity time. The longer program time gives Hahn the freedom to plan more involved activities, making the programs more worthwhile on many levels. To learn more about what's happening at the Bethel Park Public Library, visit http://bethelparkhomeschoolhappenings.blogspot.com.

children and teens to engage in more academic types of discussions with peers at their age and ability levels. Book groups serve this purpose nicely, and they also encourage reading and give children who love reading an opportunity to connect with others who share their interests. As with other programs, book groups can take many forms. Librarians should work with their homeschooling community when deciding what age levels to target with their groups (lower elementary, upper elementary, teen, and parent-child groups are common), what days and times work best, and what types of books to discuss. It is almost always a good idea to give participants at least some power over book selection when running a book group, but librarians may consider discussing a book or two that feature homeschoolers (see box on the following page).

> **RESOURCES**
>
> ## *Fiction Featuring Homeschooling*
>
> *Alice, I Think,* by Susan Juby (ages twelve and up)
>
> *Ida B . . . and Her Plans to Maximize Fun, Avoid Disaster, and (Possibly) Save the World,* by Katherine Hannigan (ages ten to fourteen)
>
> *Surviving the Applewhites,* by Stephanie S. Tolan (ages eleven and up)
>
> *What Would Joey Do?* by Jack Gantos (ages ten to fourteen)

Curriculum Swaps

Libraries can also host curriculum swaps. Many homeschoolers have learning materials they are no longer using, and many are also looking for low-cost or used materials for future use. A swap gives homeschoolers the opportunity to trade items they no longer need for items they do. Hosting a swap may be as simple as offering the use of the meeting room. Many areas have established curriculum swap events but may be willing and eager to hold the event at the library. In other areas, homeschoolers may serve as volunteers to put one together. In any case, hosting a curriculum swap can provide a valuable service for many types of homeschoolers while also increasing the library's profile in the homeschooling community.

Displays

One of the most common suggestions I hear from homeschoolers all over the country is that libraries should make space available to display homeschoolers' work. Although this isn't exactly a program, it is a valuable service. Using a bulletin board or display case to display local homeschoolers' creations brings homeschoolers into the library, increases public awareness of homeschooling, and gives the library something interesting to display to boot. This also gives homeschooled children and teens an opportunity to share their ideas with those outside their families and immediate circles. Libraries that want to do more than displays could host a homeschooling science or history fair. Homeschoolers don't get the kinds of opportunities to display their work those attending institutional schools do, so this is a valuable service most libraries can easily provide.

Preparing for College

Many homeschoolers have concerns about college admissions and how homeschooling might impact their children's postsecondary educational opportunities. Some parents start asking questions even while their children are relatively young. Libraries should certainly invest in some of the many resources that address how homeschoolers can best prepare themselves for college, but libraries that serve larger populations can also host events on the topic. Ideas include inviting an admissions officer from a local college to present information or having representatives from several colleges staff tables at a homeschooling college fair. Homeschoolers may also be particularly interested in any programs your library offers on topics such as preparing for the SAT, writing college application essays, and searching for information on scholarships and grants.

Creative librarians who have a rapport with their homeschooling communities are able to design any number of programs of interest. Librarians can visit support group meetings to do booktalks, showcase materials, or provide training on developing reading skills. Libraries can host speakers to discuss educational issues and curriculums. Some parents may even be interested in lectures and workshops on parenting and daily life. As with any population, a thorough needs assessment and a little ingenuity can go a long way toward building successful programs that benefit the library and the community.

9

Building a Special Collection

Building a special collection for homeschoolers can be intimidating. Some librarians question the wisdom of creating a collection for a relatively small population, but rest assured that collections designed for homeschoolers will be used by many people who are not homeschoolers. Teachers, tutors, parents who aren't homeschooling, and students may all have an interest in materials with an educational focus. Being relatively heavy library users, homeschoolers themselves are likely to check out the same items again and again. Librarians who put time and thought into building and marketing a homeschooling collection will be delighted with how heavily it is used.

Many librarians are overwhelmed by the challenges inherent in creating homeschooling collections. One has to take a variety of philosophies, approaches, and learning styles into account. Maintaining a collection's balance can be tricky, as can selecting materials that are not reviewed in the sources most librarians rely on. Homeschooling materials are almost all produced by relatively small specialty publishers, and most of these materials are not reviewed. Manipulatives and equipment are rarely reviewed at all, even in specialty publications. These factors make building homeschooling collections challenging, but the challenges aren't insurmountable.

GATHERING INFORMATION

The first and most important step in building any new collection is to gather as much information as possible. When creating a homeschooling collection, neglecting to perform a needs assessment is particularly perilous. The first thing you should attempt is to get a handle on your homeschooling population—some idea of how many homeschoolers are in your area. In states where homeschoolers are required to report to local school districts, statistics may be available from district offices or even the state department of education. Use the ideas presented in chapter 7 to determine which organizations exist for homeschoolers in your area, their philosophical leanings, and their size. Exact numbers are not essential, but it is helpful to have a ballpark idea of how many homeschoolers are out there before deciding how much money and staff time to devote to building a collection.

The next step is to survey the local homeschooling population to determine what kinds of materials they use and may be looking for. As we discuss in chapter 7, focus groups, e-mail surveys, and written surveys distributed through either the library or local homeschooling groups yield information that provides guidance for developing collections while also generating ideas about how to connect homeschoolers to existing materials they aren't finding. The idea here isn't to get a title-by-title list of everything homeschoolers might be looking for but rather to get a sense of what they need. Topics you might ask about include number and age of children, homeschooling philosophy/approach, preferred curriculum/material suppliers, subjects of interest, and formats of interest.

Be prepared to get a wide variety of answers to your questions and even answers that seem to be in direct contradiction with each other. Know at the outset that you aren't going to meet all the needs of all your homeschoolers. As with any other population, what you are really looking for are ways to meet the needs of the widest number of people in a way that is cost effective.

CREATING A COLLECTION STATEMENT

Once you have gathered and compiled your data, the next step is to spend some time thinking about the kind of collection you want to create, which may mean writing a formal or informal collection statement. This statement should take your library's collection development policy into account and could very well be formally incorporated into that policy. In any case, writing a collection statement helps you focus on how you are going to build your collection and what you hope to achieve. The statement should address the collection's goals as well as the types of materials that will and will not be included. Be sure to address age levels, formats, and the relative size of the collection. The statement need be only a paragraph or two long to be useful; see the Webster Public Library box for a sample.

Webster Public Library: Homeschooling Collection Statement

The Webster Public Library's homeschooling collection is a subset of the Parents' Collection. As such, it will contain materials aimed at parents or materials specifically designed for parents to use with children in preschool through grade 5 (or equivalent) for homeschooling purposes. The collection focuses on materials produced for the homeschooling market but will occasionally include materials about teaching and learning geared toward a wider audience. Materials aimed at children will be classified in the appropriate section of the children's collections.

The Children's Department intends to add 10–20 items to this collection each year. New materials will be selected based on:

- patron demand and requests,
- reviews and recommendations in homeschooling periodicals,
- reviews and recommendations in books about homeschooling, and
- reviews and recommendations in standard library review sources (*SLJ, PW, Booklist,* etc.).

Donations will be handled in accordance with the library's Collection Development Policy and the standards expressed in this statement. The Children's Department will take special care to ensure that a variety of philosophies and viewpoints are represented in the collection. Materials will be weeded when they are superseded by new editions, prove to be outdated, or become damaged.

A NOTE ON HOUSING A HOMESCHOOLING COLLECTION

Where libraries decide to shelve homeschooling materials depends on such factors as the size of the collection, the types of materials, the library's size and layout, and the composition of the library's homeschooling population. Materials of particular interest to homeschoolers can wind up interspersed throughout the library, making them difficult to find for casual browsers. For this reason, many libraries put their materials specifically for homeschoolers in a special collection, perhaps in the children's area, near special collections for parents and teachers, or in the adult area of the library. Other libraries create distinctive spine labels to help homeschoolers identify materials as they peruse the collection. Still other libraries use pathfinders and brochures to help homeschoolers locate available materials. Libraries that are most successful at connecting homeschoolers with available materials use more than one approach.

PERIODICALS

Periodicals are some of the least expensive and perhaps most helpful resources libraries can invest in. The bibliography provides a selected annotated list of periodicals aimed at homeschoolers and is an excellent place to start. In addition to being a resource for homeschoolers, most homeschooling magazines provide their readers with announcements and reviews of homeschooling materials that can help librarians build and maintain collections. It is important to remember that each magazine has its own perspective, which colors its reviews and to some degree defines its audience, but perusing these periodicals on a regular basis helps keep librarians up to date on the latest in homeschooling resources and trends.

Although it is tempting to concentrate on periodicals focused on homeschooling, homeschoolers may find periodicals on other, related topics of equal interest. Journals such as *Book Links* (www.ala.org/booklinks/) and *Teaching Pre K–8* (www.teachingk-8.com) provide information useful to parents designing their own curriculums. *Exceptional Parent Magazine* (www.eparent.com) may be of interest to those homeschooling children with special needs. Periodicals with a subject-oriented focus, such as *Cobblestone, Dig,* or *Muse* (www.cobblestonepub.com), can provide ideas for parents and enrichment for children. Magazines such as *Magic Dragon* (www.magicdragonmagazine.com) and *Teen Ink* (http://teenink.com) give homeschoolers and other youth a potential outlet for their work. Many libraries already subscribe to these periodicals; the trick is to use shelving, signage, or other means to ensure that homeschoolers can find them.

BOOKS

When people think of libraries, they think of books, and at the very least libraries should ensure that they have access to a core collection of specialized materials for their homeschooling population. The bibliography offers a core collection of titles that includes items geared specifically toward homeschoolers as well as titles such as Alfie Kohn's *Punished by Rewards* that are not written for homeschoolers but tend to be of great interest to them. Again, it's important to strive for balance in the collection by carefully selecting books that represent a variety of viewpoints and philosophies. It is worth noting that many of these books also offer reviews and recommendations for resources useful to librarians intending to branch into other specialized collections that include materials such as manipulatives, teaching aids, curriculums, catalogs, software, and subject kits.

CURRICULUM AND SUPPLY CATALOGS

A collection of curriculum and supply catalogs is a tremendously useful resource libraries can provide to homeschoolers. One of the most daunting tasks many beginning homeschoolers face is figuring out what kinds of materials to invest in, and having a ready supply of catalogs for patrons to browse can be a help. Building this collection is as easy as calling or e-mailing to request a catalog and, if possible, get on a company's mailing list. Many companies, especially smaller ones, rely on websites and no longer produce print catalogs. In these cases, librarians can print representative samples from company websites to include in the catalog collection, create a handout listing company names and websites, or create a library web page that links to company websites. The "Catalogs of Interest to Homeschoolers" box lists high-interest catalogs currently in print. Librarians can identify additional companies through feedback from homeschoolers, information obtained at curriculum fairs or conferences, or books and periodicals devoted to homeschooling (such as Cathy Duffy's *100 Top Picks for Homeschool Curriculum*). Libraries can circulate print catalogs or make them available as reference materials for in-house use.

RESOURCES

Catalogs of Interest to Homeschoolers

A Beka Home School Catalog
877-223-5226
http://www.abeka.org

Alpha Omega Publications Homeschool Catalog
800-622-3070
http://www.aop.com/homeschool/

BJU Press Total Homeschool Solutions
800-845-5731
http://www.bjupress.com

Beautiful Feet Books Catalog
800-889-1978
http://www.bfbooks.com

Calvert School Education Services Catalog
888-487-4652
http://www.calvertschool.org

Catholic Heritage Curricula Catalog
800-490-7713
http://www.chcweb.com

Chinaberry Catalog
888-481-6744
http://www.chinaberry.com

Christian Liberty Press Guide to Curriculum and Services Catalog
800-832-2741
http://www.christianlibertypress.com

Educators Publishing Service Pre-K–12 Catalog
800-225-5750
http://www.epsbooks.com

Lakeshore Learning Materials Early Childhood Catalog and Elementary Catalog
800-428-4414
http://www.lakeshorelearning.com

Loyola Press School Catalog
800-621-1008
http://www.loyolapress.org

My Father's World Preschool thru Grade 8 Catalog
573-426-4600
http://www.mfwbooks.com

Scholastic Early and Primary Reading Catalog
800-724-6527
http://www.scholastic.com/prek3catalog/

Sonlight Curriculum Catalog
303-730-6292
http://www.sonlight.com

In either case, patrons will use catalogs to gather information and ideas, and librarians may find that these resources help them develop other areas of their homeschooling collections.

TEACHING AIDS, EQUIPMENT, AND MANIPULATIVES

One of the most challenging tasks homeschoolers, parents, and others who work with children and teens face is identifying and obtaining learning materials that are effective for particular individuals in specific situations. Manipulatives, realia, games, models, and the like can be tremendously useful teaching and learning tools, or they can be a complete waste of time and money. So much depends on the quality of the item in question as well as the interests, learning styles, and teaching styles of the individuals involved. Most homeschooling parents can tell you stories about money they wish they hadn't spent on particular materials. Another challenge of these types of learning tools is that they can be pricey and, even if they are extremely useful, may be outside the family's budget or not worth the cost if they're going to be used only for a short time or by only one child. To cope with this, many homeschoolers participate in exchanges and purchase used materials, but library collections can fill this need in a way that is systematic, organized, and efficient.

Libraries that collect teaching aids give homeschoolers and others who work with youth an opportunity to explore a variety of materials to find the things that work best for their learners. They also give families access to things they might not otherwise see. Libraries can stock these collections by purchasing new materials, but they should also consider accepting donations of gently used materials from area homeschoolers. Many homeschoolers would welcome the opportunity to see things they've invested in getting used by other families. Packaging and housing these materials can take some thought, but there are solutions to most problems. For inspiration, see this chapter's profile of the Johnsburg Public Library District's Homeschool Resource Center. If undertaken with the guidance of a carefully considered donation policy and collection statement, this can be a useful way for libraries to build and expand their offerings.

CURRICULUM KITS

Curriculum kits designed by librarians can be an unusual but helpful and interesting way to fill several homeschooling needs. When homeschoolers use the library, they may be looking for materials to design their own curriculums or unit studies, materials to supplement prepackaged curriculums, or materials to tie in to the family's current interests. They often seek materials that look at a subject in a variety of ways to reinforce facts and concepts, to accommodate different learning styles, and perhaps to explore the same topic with more than one child.

Identifying and pulling together multidisciplinary and multimedia materials on a topic from more than one area of the collection can be a challenge for staff and homeschoolers alike. Curriculum kits bring together a variety of materials on the same topic in a convenient package that is ready to be checked out. A kit might include any number of items—fiction and nonfiction books, activity guides, films, charts, manipulatives, basic equipment, games. Kits are normally packaged in something along the lines of a hanging bag, tote bag, backpack, or box. They are most useful when they are housed in something sturdy and are prominently labeled with the topic, target age level, and contents. This is an excellent way for librarians to use their specialized knowledge of youth development and materials to create learning packages which, if properly promoted and displayed, will be heavily used by homeschoolers and non-homeschoolers alike.

Sample Curriculum Kit: Insects (Grades K–2)

Bugs Are Insects, by Anne Rockwell (nonfiction book)

Look Closer: An Introduction to Bug-Watching, by Gay Holland (activity guide)

Ace Lacewing, Bug Detective, by David Biedrzycki (picture book/fiction)

All about Bugs (DVD)

3-inch magnifying glass

Sample Curriculum Kit: Birds (Grades 3–5)

Birds: Nature's Magnificent Flying Machines, by Caroline Arnold (nonfiction)

Raptor! A Kid's Guide to Birds of Prey, by Christyna M. Laubach (nonfiction)

Field Trips, by Jim Aronsky (activity guide)

Project Ultraswan, by Elinor Osborn (nonfiction, profile of scientists doing research)

Songbirds: The Language of Song, by Sylvia A. Johnson (nonfiction)

Birding by Ear: Eastern and Central North America (CD and booklet)

PROFILE

Johnsburg Public Library District's Homeschool Resource Center

The Johnsburg Public Library is a 10,000-square-foot building chartered to serve a population of about 12,000 people in a rural community in Illinois, not far from the Wisconsin border. It seems an unlikely place to find a homeschooler's dream library—one that collects and circulates homeschooling magazines, curriculum materials, educational games, kits, and science equipment. Their Homeschool Resource Center does just that, though, and so much more.

Even though Johnsburg is a small community, the area has a sizable homeschooling population. The library didn't suspect the true size of the population, though, until local homeschooling mother Kathy Wentz stopped in several years ago to drop off pamphlets listing the names and contact information for the ten homeschooling groups then active in the county. This began a conversation between Wentz and librarian Maria Zawacki that led Wentz to reveal her idea about creating a library collection where homeschoolers could borrow much-needed educational materials. Zawacki liked the idea, and a $55,000 Library Services and Technology Act Grant through the Illinois State Library helped make Wentz's dream into the impressive Homeschool Resource Center.

Housed in what used to be a study room, the Center includes materials geared toward teaching youth of all ages, even preschoolers. The collection spans and accommodates a full range of philosophies and approaches, and it contains a wealth of materials very few libraries collect and circulate—games, kits, and equipment. Many items have dozens of pieces. They circulate a set of Cuisenaire rods, for example, that has 155 pieces. They have telescopes, microscopes, and even prepared slides. The Center has curriculum materials from producers favored by homeschoolers, including A Beka Book, Singapore Math, Alpha Omega, and Rosetta Stone. Everything is available on a six-week loan to anyone who walks in the door.

To busy public librarians, this kind of collection sounds like a potential nightmare: How does one store atypical items? What about cataloging? What about damage and loss?

"Two of my biggest fears when applying for this grant back in 2001 were how the staff was going to deal with it and how the items were going to hold up," says Maria Zawacki, but she and Kathy Wentz agree that it has all gone more smoothly than they could have hoped. Zawacki attributes much of the Center's success to Wentz. She says that it is essential to have someone who knows the homeschooling community, has a broad perspective, and can help the library select items that are truly useful. As a volunteer, Wentz has gone the extra mile to promote and help maintain the collection.

Wentz herself attributes the overall success of the Center to planning, purchasing classroom-quality equipment instead of the least expensive, keeping copies of instructions on file, holding on to "extra" pieces that might be useful as replacements, and displaying items on similar topics near each other rather than sticking to a strictly Dewey order or separating items by format. A former classroom teacher herself, Wentz spends about an hour a week maintaining the collection, including identifying new items to add, shelf reading, and replacing parts and batteries. The Center also takes donations from homeschoolers, which she sorts through to determine what to add to the collection, what to use as replacements, and what to sell in the Annual HRC Open House and Used Curriculum Flea Market. Wentz says that most lost and damaged items are easy to replace (dice, cardboard boxes, etc.) and that none of the more expensive items such as microscopes or telescopes have been damaged.

Overall, Wentz says, "I can easily see a day when a collection such as this is in every county/parish of almost every state. The collections should be full of ideal resources for every teacher in every situation—public or private, large or small." She sees these collections as useful for teachers and any parent as well as homeschoolers. Indeed, both Kathy Wentz and Maria Zawacki report that their Homeschool Resource Center has seen use from an amazing array of people, including teachers, some of whom drive lengthy distances to utilize this unique and tremendously valuable collection.

10

Helping Homeschoolers in the Library: It's Easier Than You Think

In this final chapter, I give libraries that are just beginning to work with homeschoolers and libraries that are not ready to devote a great deal of resources to homeschoolers a list of ten low-cost ideas to start them on the path of providing better services. Libraries that try even a few of the items on this list will go a long way toward letting homeschoolers know that they are welcome in the library and that librarians are interested in helping them—these are, truly, the most important things. Then I show you how one library system has approached serving homeschoolers through a cooperative grant project. As a final inspiration, I close with an interview with homeschooling mother Amy McCarthy, a woman who has great ideas for homeschoolers and librarians alike.

THE TEN EASIEST THINGS YOUR LIBRARY CAN DO TO SERVE HOMESCHOOLERS

1. When you see parents with school-age kids in the library in the middle of the day, take some time to talk to them and find out if they're homeschoolers. Introduce yourself. Ask what they're working on. Recognizing these patrons and developing relationships with them will be key to any program you develop. (Learn more about the benefits of talking to homeschoolers in chapter 7.)

2. Make sure people can find homeschooling materials in the library. Many libraries have materials of particular interest to homeschoolers spread throughout the library: magazines in the magazine collection, books for parents in parenting or adult collections, books geared toward teaching children in the children's room, books for teens divided between the adult's and children's collections. Consider setting aside a few shelves for materials devoted to homeschooling, and be sure to highlight the area with clear signage. Other options for making sure patrons can find available materials include spine labels or pathfinders. It does no good to purchase materials for homeschoolers unless they can find them. (Learn more about creating collections to meet homeschoolers' needs in chapter 9.)

3. Learn about homeschooling groups active in your community, what their missions are and who is running them. Make information about these groups available to other homeschoolers through a brochure or by keeping the organizations' materials on hand. Connect with leaders of local groups to find out if they are willing to promote library programs. (Learn more about connecting with local groups in chapter 7.)

4. Allow and encourage homeschoolers to use library meeting room space. I have talked with dozens of homeschoolers all over the country, and almost all of them have expressed the need for an inexpensive or no-cost place for groups to hold meetings. I have heard about libraries that bar homeschoolers from using meeting rooms either directly or through inordinately high room usage fees. Allowing homeschooling groups to meet in the library is one of the easiest ways libraries can build a positive relationship with the homeschooling community and provide a highly needed service to some of their heaviest borrowers. (Learn more about homeschooling groups in chapter 7.)

5. Display projects created by homeschooled children and teens. This is the second-most common service homeschoolers have told me they wish their libraries would offer, and it is so easy for libraries to do. (Learn more about other programs for homeschoolers in chapter 8.)

6. Create handouts that list your state's laws pertaining to homeschoolers. Remember that laws vary widely from state to state, and, as with any other legal issue, librarians should make sure that they hand out current information and never offer legal interpretations. (Learn more about laws pertaining to homeschoolers in chapter 1.)

7. Maintain a file of catalogs from companies that sell materials and supplies of interest to homeschoolers. These could circulate or be available for reference use. (Learn more about companies that cater to homeschoolers in chapter 9.)
8. Allow homeschoolers to apply for an extended loan period, usually the equivalent of twice the regular loan period for books (e.g., if your library loans books for three weeks, allow homeschoolers to borrow them for six). (Learn more about homeschoolers and how they use the library in chapter 1.)
9. Consider the needs of homeschoolers when creating policies about interlibrary loan fees. Remember that homeschoolers often rely heavily on being able to borrow materials from more than one library.
10. Attend local homeschooling conferences, lectures, and curriculum fairs. You will learn about new resources, have an opportunity to talk to vendors, and connect with more homeschoolers in your service area. (Learn more about homeschooling events in chapter 7.)

PROFILE

Monroe County's "Serving Homeschoolers" Grant

The Monroe County Library System is a federation of independent public libraries located throughout Monroe County, New York. According to statistics from the New York State Office for Reporting and Technology, there were 1,622 homeschooled children in the county in the 2003/4 academic year. This is a sizable population, and one spread throughout the county libraries' service areas, making it difficult for any one library to commit large amounts of effort and resources to serving homeschoolers. In the fall of 2004, four Monroe County libraries decided to work together to provide better services to homeschoolers in the county as a whole. The result was the 2005–2007 New York State Library's Parent and Child Services Grant, "Serving Homeschoolers."

To start, the librarians from each of the libraries identified homeschoolers in their communities and invited them to a focus group meeting designed to gather information about how well public libraries were serving the county's homeschoolers and what libraries could do to improve services. Among other things, the homeschoolers in attendance expressed interest in seeing stronger homeschooling collections, more nonfiction DVDs, and library skills classes for homeschoolers. The librarians used this information to create a grant program (see the appendix for the complete grant application), which they were awarded in July 2005.

The notion behind the grant was that none of these four libraries could provide first-rate services for homeschoolers individually, but by working cooperatively they could make much more of an impact on services to homeschoolers. The grant provided funds to hire a half-time librarian who oversaw building partnerships with local homeschooling groups and coordinated grant activities. Each library created its own homeschooling collection that included books on homeschooling, curriculum and supply catalogs, homeschooling laws, and pathfinders on topics of particular interest to homeschoolers (fire prevention, New York state history, Christian fiction, etc.). Each library also developed a particular subject specialty and worked to develop its regular collections in this area (focusing on AV) while also using grant funds to build sixty curriculum kits for children in grades K–5 that focused on subtopics within their subject. The libraries also worked together to create and cross-promote library skills classes on different subjects in different months, with the idea that homeschoolers could attend classes at more than one library if they wished.

In the end, the participating libraries were able to make more of an impact collectively than they would have individually. They shared curriculums and ideas for classes, they benefited from consultations with each other while creating their curriculum kits, and they referred homeschoolers to the other libraries for items of interest. Library skills classes were well attended, and the homeschooling collections and curriculum kits have been used heavily by homeschoolers and non-homeschoolers alike. The partnerships these libraries forged with each other and with the homeschooling community have shown how successful services to homeschoolers can be and hold the promise of building more partnerships and stronger services to homeschoolers in the coming years.

PROFILE

Amy McCarthy

"I was working part-time in the circulation department of the Guilderland Public Library when I discovered homeschooling," says homeschooling mother and brand-new librarian Amy McCarthy. McCarthy hadn't even heard of homeschooling when daughters Kate and Madeline were toddlers and she started noticing books on homeschooling in the return pile. McCarthy says she's a rule follower, and "it took a long time to convince myself that I could do this." By the time Kate was old enough to start kindergarten, mom was ready.

McCarthy and her husband have taken an eclectic approach to homeschooling their daughters (now ages eight and ten). They use workbooks for subjects such as spelling and math, and they have done unit studies when appropriate. The family is involved in activities through a local homeschooling support group, which McCarthy calls "instrumental in our homeschooling journey." Her children participate in other organized activities such as soccer, Irish step dancing, piano lessons, and art classes. They also enjoy trips to museums, historical sites, and plays.

Amy McCarthy recently finished six and a half years of part-time study at the University at Albany (New York) to earn her MSIS degree. As part of her studies, she brought her personal and professional lives together in an internship at Guilderland Public Library, the same library where she first learned about homeschooling. As part of that project, she worked on the library's homeschooling collection, paring it down before moving it to a new location in the library. She created a draft collection development policy, weeded the collection, moved materials that didn't belong there to other collections, and recommended items to purchase to round out the collection and bring it up to date. Thus far, she reports, this is the only collection of its kind in the Upper Hudson Library System.

Also as a student, McCarthy worked on a *JLAMS* article with professor Deborah Lines Andersen titled "Homeschoolers at the Public Library: Are Library Services and Policies Keeping Pace?"[1] The article explores the relationship between homeschoolers and libraries in the Capital District of New York State. When asked why and how libraries should serve homeschoolers, McCarthy responds, "I believe homeschoolers are an untapped audience for library programming. According to the survey reported on in our article, 61 percent of homeschoolers regularly use more than one public library. Yet only 10 percent of the responding libraries reported programming aimed at homeschoolers."

McCarthy knows that any library that starts reaching out to homeschoolers will find a welcoming and helpful community. Homeschoolers rely on libraries, she points out, and "through libraries we are able to continuously stock our shelves with new and interesting books and then return them and get all new ones! What a fabulous resource!" Understanding that many public libraries are overburdened and underfunded, she suggests working with homeschoolers willing to volunteer to help set up and run programs. As an alternative to programming, she suggests displaying homeschoolers' work or extending the same special borrowing privileges to homeschoolers that libraries offer teachers in local schools. "Homeschoolers do tend to be unapologetic book freaks," she says, and homeschoolers rely on the public library for learning materials. "Libraries that serve homeschoolers well are bound to influence a future generation of library supporters." As a librarian and as a homeschooler, Amy McCarthy looks forward to the possibility of working with both groups to build services that benefit the whole community.

NOTE

1. Amy McCarthy and Deborah Lines Andersen, "Homeschoolers at the Public Library: Are Library Services and Policies Keeping Pace?" *JLAMS* 3, no. 1 (2006–2007), http://www.nyla.org/content/user_10/JLAMSspring07wg.pdf.

APPENDIX

"Serving Homeschoolers" Grant Application: New York State Library Parent and Child Library Services, 2005–2007

1. Abstract

    a. Write a brief one-paragraph synopsis of the project's purpose and target group. Do not describe activities here.

    This project is a partnership between four member libraries of the Monroe County Library System: the Webster Public Library, the Chili Public Library, the Seymour Library (Brockport), and the Parma Public Library. It seeks to provide targeted services to homeschoolers in Monroe County. By providing educational opportunities and materials to children and parents, we will make the library system an integral part of homeschoolers' routines and help parents provide higher-quality educational experiences for their children.

2. Need, Target Audience, Collaboration

    a. What is the need for this project? Who will benefit? What is the size of the target audience? How will you reach them?

    According to the New York State Office for Reporting and Technology, there were 1,622 homeschooled children in Monroe County in the 2003–2004 academic year. According to the National Center for Education Statistics, the number of homeschooled children in the U.S. grew 29% from 1999–2003, confirming the observation that homeschooling is a rising trend. All four libraries involved in this grant are serving homeschoolers and have had many comments from parents requesting materials and services not currently provided. Being outside the traditional educational framework, homeschooling families have a unique and strong need for informational resources. In December 2004, a focus group of homeschooling parents from throughout Monroe County revealed parents' frustration with their attempts to locate information. They cited the following needs:

  i. Instructional kits that would gather together a variety of materials (including print, non-print, fiction, nonfiction, and activity guides) on particular topics.
  ii. More nonfiction non-print media (including videos, DVDs, books on CD, software, and science equipment) to support instruction.
  iii. Pathfinders on frequently studied topics.
  iv. Library skills classes for students as well as adults.
  v. Outlets for their children's academic endeavors (display space, project fairs, etc.).
  vi. Longer borrowing periods.

We will reach parents and children through our personal contacts in each library and also through the major Rochester homeschooling organizations: Rochester Area Homeschoolers' Association (hereafter referred to as RAHA), Loving Education at Home (hereafter referred to as LEAH), and Catholic Homeschoolers of Western New York. We will also disseminate information through an e-mail listserv.

b. How does the project relate to the Library's long-range plan?

All four partner libraries' missions and long-range plans emphasize the importance of supporting the community's informational and educational needs (mission statements attached). This grant also supports libraries' traditional role of encouraging lifelong learning.

c. How will the project improve on current library programming?

Two of the libraries involved in this grant (Webster and Brockport) have offered programs to homeschoolers in the past with mixed results. By combining the efforts of four libraries and librarians, we will create higher-quality specialized programming that can be offered at all four locations and then, ideally, be duplicated at other libraries in the Monroe County Public Library System.

d. List project partners and cooperating organizations; outline the role of each agency in planning, implementation, and evaluation and attach letters of support.

LEAH will be our main project partner, although we will have at least one member from RAHA and one member of LEAH on our Advisory Board. LEAH is the most active homeschooling organization in the Rochester area, and they will help us distribute surveys and publicize programs and services. A letter of support is attached.

3. Project Description

a-b. What is the project's goal? List project objectives. Briefly describe the activities planned to accomplish each objective.

The project's goal is to provide educational opportunities and materials to families who homeschool, to make the library system an integral part of homeschoolers' routines, and to help parents provide higher-quality educational experiences for their children.

OBJECTIVES/ACTIVITIES

Objectives	*Activities*
Increase available information about homeschooling itself (laws, how-to guides, curriculums, etc.).	Develop a folder of information about New York State laws and regulations that apply to homeschoolers and make this available at each partner library. (August 2005, update May 2006)
	Develop a file of curriculum catalogs and sample curriculums to make available at each partner library. (August 2005, update June 2006)
	Develop a core collection list of materials about homeschooling and purchase these items for each partner library. (August 2005)

Objectives	Activities
	Design a spine label to put on homeschooling materials to make them easier to locate within the collection. (August 2005)
Increase informational materials and equipment that will support homeschooling curriculums and instruction, helping parents provide higher-quality educational experiences for their children.	Each partner library will develop a subject specialty in print and non-print media. Chili will focus on Social Studies, Brockport on Language Arts and Foreign Languages, Webster on Science and Math, and Parma on the Arts. (August 2005–December 2006)
	During each grant year, each library will develop subject-specific multimedia kits in their specialty including instructional materials designed to explore various subtopics. (August 2005–December 2006)
	Make sure each library has a children's computer with access to educational resources. (November 2005)
	Develop eight pathfinders for frequently studied topics that include information in a variety of formats. (4 in 2005–2006 academic year, 4 in 2006–2007 academic year)
	Purchase circulating science equipment to be housed at the Webster Public Library (microscope, telescope, magnifying glass, binoculars, prism). (August 2006)
Teach homeschooling families information literacy skills.	Develop four library skills classes to be offered each year of the grant. (4 in 2005–2006 academic year, 4 in 2006–2007 academic year)
	Develop a computer database class specifically for parents to offer each year of the grant. (October 2005, October 2006)

Objectives	Activities
Increase homeschooling families' connection to and use of the public library.	Hold a Science Fair for Homeschoolers. (March 2006) Create display space in all four libraries for homeschoolers' projects. (August 2005) Establish an e-mail listserv for homeschooling families and librarians to communicate with each other about materials, programs, and services. (August 2005) Create a special six-week loan period for homeschoolers at each of the four partner libraries. (August 2005)
Increase librarians' awareness of the needs of this population.	Establish a grant advisory board consisting of the Children's Librarians from the four partner libraries, the Project Coordinator, and at least four homeschooling parents from throughout the region. (July 2005) Project Coordinator and one Librarian will attend the annual LEAH Conference in Syracuse. (June 2006)

    c. Provide a time-line of project activities.

July 2005

- Establish grant Advisory Board.
- Advisory Board hires Project Coordinator.

August 2005

- Project Coordinator develops folders of information about New York State laws and regulations that apply to homeschoolers.
- Project Coordinator develops files of curriculum catalogs and sample curriculums.
- The Children's Librarians at the four partner libraries order core collections of homeschooling materials.
- Project Coordinator creates homeschooling spine label.

- Project Coordinator establishes and advertises an e-mail listserv for homeschooling families and librarians to communicate with each other about materials, programs, and services.
- Each library creates a special 6-week loan period for homeschoolers.
- Project coordinator distributes, collects, and tallies e-mail survey of homeschooling parents.

September 2005

- Project Coordinator and Children's Librarians begin developing 30 subject kits for each library.
- Project Coordinator begins designing four library skills classes in conjunction with Children's Librarians.
- Project Coordinator begins designing database class for parents in conjunction with Children's Librarians.
- Each library creates homeschooling areas in the libraries, which will include display space where space allows.

October 2005

- Project Coordinator publishes first pathfinder.
- Library skills class offered at Chili Public Library.
- Computer Databases class offered for parents in the computer lab at the Webster Public Library.

November 2005

- Library skills class offered at Parma Public Library.
- Project Coordinator purchases computers and equipment for Parma and Chili Public Libraries.

December 2005

- The 30 subject kits are processed and available at each library.
- Project Coordinator publishes second pathfinder.

February 2006

- The Project Coordinator publishes third pathfinder.

March 2006

- Library skills class offered at Webster Public Library.
- All 120 first-year subject kits (30 at each library) are processed and available for circulation.

April 2006

- Library skills class offered at Brockport Public Library.
- Project Coordinator publishes fourth pathfinder.

May 2006

- Project Coordinator updates folders of information about New York State laws and regulations that apply to homeschoolers.
- Project coordinator distributes, collects, and tallies follow-up e-mail survey of homeschooling parents.

June 2006 — End of Year One

- Project Coordinator updates and adds to files of curriculum catalogs and sample curriculums.
- Project Coordinator and one Children's Librarian attend LEAH Conference in Syracuse.

August 2006

- Purchase circulating science equipment.

September 2006

- Children's Librarians and Project Coordinator begin developing 30 additional subject kits for each library.
- Children's Librarians purchase supplemental materials in subject specialties.

October 2006

- Project Coordinator publishes fifth pathfinder.
- Library skills class offered at Chili Public Library.
- Computer Databases class offered for parents in the computer lab at the Webster Public Library.

November 2006

- Library skills class offered at Parma Public Library.

December 2006

- Project Coordinator publishes sixth pathfinder.

February 2007

- Project Coordinator publishes seventh pathfinder.

March 2007

- Science Fair.
- Library skills class offered at Webster Public Library.
- All 120 first-year subject kits (30 at each library) are processed and available for circulation.

April 2007

- Project Coordinator publishes eighth pathfinder.
- Library skills class offered at Brockport Public Library.

May 2007

- Project coordinator distributes, collects, and tallies follow-up e-mail survey of homeschooling parents.

4. Budget Narrative
   a. In narrative form, explain the importance of each budget item and how it contributes to the project purpose.

   Our largest expenditure each year of the grant will be the $22,930 to hire a half-time Project Coordinator. This Librarian will be essential to the success of the grant. He or she will do much of the labor-intensive upfront work that will provide the basis of our services to homeschoolers during the two years of the grant and in the years beyond. In consultation with the Advisory Board, the Project Coordinator will design the library skills classes as well as the subject kits. He or she will create, design, and publish the pathfinders. He or she will establish the files of NYS laws that apply to homeschoolers as well as curriculum catalogs and sample curriculums. He or she will conduct classes during the two years of the grant, be heavily involved in publicity and communication, and will also be responsible for gathering evaluative data and writing grant reports. The Project Coordinator will, thus, be involved in all the grant's objectives. We are also requesting $105 each year to cover this person's travel from library to library. A job description for this position is attached.

The second-largest expenditure each year will be for library materials. We are asking for $10,800 each year to create a combined total of 240 circulating subject kits. This figure includes the cost of all processing supplies. These kits are what homeschooling parents ask for over and over and will be the keystone of our project. Two sample kit descriptions are attached. We are asking for an additional $3000 during the second year of the grant to allow each library to purchase supplemental circulating materials within their subject specialties. The subject kits will be an excellent resource, but, during the focus group, parents expressed their desire to see general collections strengthened. By creating a specialty at each participating library, parents will know that they can go to particular libraries and expect an extraordinary collection of materials in a particular subject. We are also asking for $1000 in the first year of the grant to establish core collections of materials about homeschooling and $120 each year to subscribe to homeschooling magazines. This will ensure that parents who homeschool have access to quality information about how to homeschool. In the second year of the grant, we're requesting $400 for circulating science equipment such as telescopes, microscopes, etc. Again, this is a need parents cited in the focus group. The cost of getting such equipment is prohibitive to many families, but they are essential for quality educational opportunities.

We are requesting $3800 in the first year to ensure that the two libraries that don't already have computers with educational software (Parma and Chili) can have them. Many homeschoolers do not have up-to-date computers with educational software at home, so this will make an excellent shared resource for them and provide an additional reason to visit the library.

We are requesting additional funds to create display spaces for homeschoolers' projects in each library and also to ensure that each library has a computer with educational software. We are requesting $300 to host a Science Fair during the second year of the grant that will include projects done by homeschoolers as well as a presentation by the Rochester Museum and Science Center on a scientific topic. These activities will satisfy homeschoolers' need to present some of their work, give homeschooling parents a chance to network and get ideas, provide high-quality educational experiences, and also to strengthen homeschoolers' connection to libraries. Last, we are requesting $600 to send the Project Coordinator and one Librarian to the annual LEAH conference in Syracuse, New York. This will give the Project Coordinator and Librarian an opportunity to learn more about homeschooling and network with curriculum and materials vendors.

According to the American Association of School Librarians (division of ALA), schools spend an average of $21 per student annually on library materials. Our project will spend an average of about $24 in grant funds per homeschooled student in Monroe County each year on materials and services. This seems to be a reasonable investment in a population that has such a pressing need for information and services and also has the potential to be heavy lifelong library users.

- **b.** List the dollar amount and source of other funds or in-kind services, provided by the applicant and any partner, to be used to carry out the project.

    $41,600—Staff time provided by each library. (Average of 5 hrs./week for each Children's Librarian at an average rate of $20/hour.)

    $600—Staff time provided by each library to process materials.

    $300—Incidental expenses such as paper, toner, and faxing provided by each library for program publicity.

5. Evaluation/Outcomes

    a-b. *What* will you measure to provide quantitative data about your project's service or product outputs? *How* will you measure the outputs?

What	How
Number of children and adults attending library skills and computer database classes.	Attendance lists.
Number of children and adults participating in the Science Fair.	Attendance lists.
Number of circulations for multimedia kits.	Check circulation statistics in LMS for kits at the end of each grant year.
Number of pathfinders distributed.	Keep statistics on how many pathfinders are copied. At the end of each grant year, subtract the number that haven't been handed out/taken to determine the number that have been taken/used.
Number of homeschoolers' displays.	Each library should keep track of what is being displayed in the library and how long it stays up.

c-d. *What* will you measure to show the outcomes or impact of your services or products on the identified target population? *How* will you measure the outcomes?

What	How
Children will have increased information literacy skills.	Have a pre- and post-test at each library skills class to assess the amount of knowledge children gained.
Families will know more about using the library and will use it more.	Distribute an e-mail survey at the beginning of year one. Distribute the same survey at the end of year one and the end of year two to monitor progress.

6. Continuation Plans and Statewide Dissemination of Project Results
   a. Briefly describe how, if successful, this project will be continued after the grant project ends. Include information on partners and sources of funding.

   > Each library will commit part of its normal materials budget each year to maintaining and expanding on subject specialties and subject kits. Pathfinders, files of legal information, and curriculum files will be maintained cooperatively by staff at each library. Established library skills classes will continue to be offered cooperatively on an annual basis. Existing staff will commit time and funds to these projects.

   b. Please indicate below how you and your project partners will share information with libraries and other interested organizations in New York State about the project results.

   X   Library or system web site: Project events will be publicized on individual libraries' web sites, the MCLS web site, and kidsoutandabout.com.

   X   NYLA presentation, poster session, sharing session: We will volunteer to present a Table Talk at NYLA on library services to homeschoolers. Class materials and pathfinders will be made available to all attendees.

   X   Library system or other professional meetings: We will present our project and results at an MCLS Children's Librarians' meeting. We will make class materials and pathfinders available to all system libraries.

   X   Articles in newsletters, journals, etc.: We will make every attempt to publish an article on our project in the *YSS Newsletter*, *Children and Libraries* (the ALSC journal) and/or *School Library Journal*.

PROJECT COORDINATOR

Position Description

This half-time Librarian will be responsible for coordinating the 2005–2007 "Serving Homeschoolers" NYS Parent and Child Services Grant and will be heavily involved in most project activities.

Minimum Qualifications

Graduation from an accredited college or university with an MLS degree.

Skills and Abilities

1. Open, friendly, creative, and child-engaging personality
2. Solid knowledge of child development
3. Comfortable working with and leading groups of children and adults
4. Ability to instruct patrons
5. Decision-making ability
6. Ability to learn computer software applications relevant to job duties
7. Ability to express ideas clearly and accurately both orally and in writing
8. Good judgment
9. Initiative, tact, and courtesy in dealing with the staff and public
10. Physical condition commensurate with the demands of the position

Major Duties

1. Coordinates "Serving Homeschoolers" NYS Parent and Child Services Grant.
2. Responsible for all grant-related statistics, evaluations, and reporting.
3. Promotes all programs and services for homeschoolers through a variety of media, including an electronic listserv.
4. Plans and conducts library skills classes for children and parents who homeschool.

5. Establish and maintain files of NYS laws and regulations that apply to homeschoolers.
6. Establish and maintain files of curriculum catalogs and samples.
7. Create pathfinders on a variety of subjects.
8. Creates multimedia instructional subject kits for homeschoolers, in consultation with Children's Librarians.
9. Assists Children's Librarians in other grant-related activities.

MISSION STATEMENTS

Chili Public Library

The Chili Public Library, using its own resources and those of the Monroe County Library System, provides materials and services to assist community residents in meeting their personal, educational, professional and recreational information needs. The Library places special emphasis on assisting students and on stimulating enthusiasm of young children for reading and learning. The Chili Public Library, through its staff and Board of Trustees, will maintain an innovative, cost-effective and responsible group of services and materials in order to meet its objectives and to provide its patrons with convenient and maximum opportunity for self-service.

Seymour Library (Brockport)

The mission of the Seymour Library is to provide a wide variety of materials to meet the public's informational and recreational needs with the aid of a professional library staff.

The Seymour library affirms each individual's right to free access to information.

The library seeks to preserve the locale's cultural and intellectual heritage while helping its citizens prepare for the future.

Parma Public Library

The Board of Trustees of the Parma Public Library is committed to informing, educating and enriching the life of the community through free and open access to all materials to everyone, support for the patron's right to confidentiality (Library Bill of Rights), awareness in responding to the changing needs of the community and cooperation with public and private institutions in collecting and preserving historical and cultural materials. It also supports a prudent, judicious approach to the selection and use of new technology, a firm commitment to providing competent, responsive staff and provision of a facility which is attractive, comfortable and easily accessible to its users.

Webster Public Library

The mission of the Webster Public Library is to make readily available the most wanted library materials and services to all those who use the library and to serve as an access point for information—in a welcoming and professional atmosphere.

SAMPLE ARTS KIT FOR GRADES 3–5

Topic: Monet and Impressionism

Non-Fiction Books:

Linnea in Monet's Garden, by Christina Bjork, illus. by Lina Anderson	$14.00
Monet and the Impressionists for Kids, by Carol Sabbeth	$ 17.95
What Makes a Monet a Monet? by Richard Muhlberger	$16.99

Fiction Books:

Charlotte in Paris, by Joan Knight	$16.95

A/V:

Linnea in Monet's Garden (DVD)	$14.95
Hanging Pouch + Other Processing Supplies	$ 3.00

Total: $83.84

SAMPLE SCIENCE KIT FOR GRADES K–3

Topic: Spiders and Other Arachnids

Non-Fiction Books:

About Arachnids, by Cathryn Sill, illus. by John Sill	$15.95
The Tarantula Scientist, by Sy Montgomery, illus. by Nic Bishop	$18.00
Spiders and Their Web Sites, by Margery Facklam, illus. by Alan Male	$15.95

Fiction Books:

An Interview with Harry the Tarantula, by Leigh Ann Tyson, illus. by Henrik Drescher	$15.95
The Spider and the Fly, by Mary Botham Howitt, illus. by Tony DiTerlizzi	$16.95

A/V:

Magic School Bus Creepy, Crawly Fun (DVD)	$14.97
Hanging Pouch + Other Processing Supplies	$ 3.00

Total: $100.77

GLOSSARY

Charlotte Mason homeschooling. Based on the work of British educator Charlotte Mason, this approach to homeschooling emphasizes the use of literature, focused lessons, and plenty of time outdoors.

classical homeschooling. This homeschooling method popularized by Susan Wise Bauer and Jessie Wise's *The Well-Trained Mind* is based on the medieval trivium. Classical homeschoolers are highly structured and focus on memorization, logic, history, and great literature.

Cuisenaire rods. A series of colored bars of different lengths that can be used to demonstrate mathematical concepts.

curriculum. A structured plan for a course of study.

curriculum fairs. Events during which vendors sell homeschooling supplies and materials.

eclectic homeschooling. Homeschoolers who take bits and pieces of a variety of homeschooling philosophies and approaches.

giftedness. Extraordinary ability or talent.

high/low books. Books designed for reluctant or struggling readers. The books deal with topics of interest to those past the traditional beginning reader level, but they feature the controlled vocabulary, wide margins, and larger print with fewer words on a page beginning readers need.

Holt Associates. An organization founded by unschooling advocate John Holt to disseminate information and support homeschoolers.

Home School Legal Defense Association (HSLDA). Powerful conservative Protestant organization that provides members with legal assistance and actively lobbies in what they perceive to be homeschoolers' best interests.

manipulatives. Physical objects used to teach abstract concepts.

Moore Formula. A "formula" created by early homeschooling proponents Raymond and Dorothy Moore that they thought would guarantee any child a complete education: (1) study, but not too much, especially in the primary grades; (2) manual labor, which they considered as or even more important than study; and (3) service in the home and community.

multidisciplinary. Examining a topic/theme from the perspective of a variety of subjects rather than through the lens of a single subject area.

multimedia. Using a variety of formats (books, newspapers, magazines, videos, computer games, realia, manipulatives, etc.).

multiple intelligences theory. Howard Gardner's influential theory that intelligence can't be measured or described in one way.

National Home Education Research Institute (NHERI). Founded in 1990 by researcher and homeschooling advocate Brian D. Ray, this nonprofit organization researches and disseminates information pertaining to homeschooling.

pathfinder. A guide designed to assist information seekers. Pathfinders can be print or electronic and generally encompass a variety of materials.

"people first" language. Putting people before their disabilities in everyday speech and writing. For example, one would say "a child who has autism" rather than "an autistic child."

phonics. A system of teaching reading skills that involves teaching the sounds associated with particular letters and letter combinations.

radical unschooling. A segment of the unschooling population who believes that parents should not direct or influence their children's learning in any way. Some people refer to themselves proudly as "radical" unschoolers while others use this as a derogatory term.

realia. "Real" objects used for educational purposes (examples include leaves, dried flowers, tools, etc.).

school-at-home. A phrase frequently used to refer to homeschoolers who re-create the structures and routines of institutional schools in their homes.

teen advisory boards. A group of teenage volunteers that meets on a regular basis to help build and improve library services.

trivium. Learning model derived from medieval schools in which students focused on subjects in three distinct stages, the first being grammar/memorization, the second logic, and the third rhetoric. Today this model is used by classical homeschoolers.

twice exceptional. A phrase referring to children who exhibit traits of both a learning disability and giftedness.

unit studies. A teaching and learning model in which students spend a period of time exploring a particular topic in depth from a multidisciplinary perspective.

unschooling. An approach to homeschooling advocated by educational theorist John Holt that emphasizes child-led learning.

whole language. A system of teaching reading that focuses on immersing learners in literature and language.

BIBLIOGRAPHY

BOOKS

The following resources are divided into five main categories. "General Homeschooling Resources" are titles that provide guidance, advice, and tips to a broad range of homeschoolers. "Homeschooling Philosophies" includes books that explain or have influenced various lines of thought within the homeschooling movement. "Faith-Based Homeschooling" are resources geared specifically toward homeschoolers of particular faiths. "Homeschooling Children with Special Needs" covers titles that deal with homeschooling children who have learning disabilities, giftedness, or other less typical learning issues. "Professional Resources" is a collection of titles that can assist library professionals as they begin to work toward better serving their homeschooling populations, subdivided into "Collection Development," "Program Development," and "Teen Services."

It goes without saying that there are any number of ways one could categorize a list and that many titles could appear in more than one category. The annotations should provide further insight into each title's intended audience, scope, and perspective. Additionally, sources tagged with an asterisk would make an ideal core collection for libraries serving active homeschooling populations.

General Homeschooling Resources

*Armstrong, Thomas. *In Their Own Way: Discovering and Encouraging Your Child's Multiple Intelligences.* New York: J. P. Tarcher/Putnam, 2000.

Armstrong's interpretation of Howard Gardner's theory of multiple intelligences is a favorite among homeschoolers as well as college students, teachers, and parents who send their children to institutional schools. Most books about homeschooling offer some kind of information about learning styles, but this basic book-length treatment of the subject will be welcome in most collections.

*Bailey, Guy. *The Ultimate Homeschool Physical Education Game Book.* Camas, WA: Educators Press, 2003.

In this unique resource, Bailey emphasizes the ways physical activities contribute to overall learning and the ability to live a healthy and productive life. Activities are designed to build skills, maximize participation, work with small groups, and utilize minimal equipment. Bailey devotes equal time to building the skills necessary to play team sports such as soccer and basketball and those necessary for such nonteam sports as golf and jump roping. Many of his games can be tied into other subjects such as math and science and will prove useful to a wide range of homeschoolers.

*Barfield, Rhonda. *Real-Life Homeschooling: The Stories of 21 Families Who Teach Their Children at Home.* New York: Fireside, 2002.

As the title indicates, the book profiles twenty-one homeschooling families with a wide variety of styles and beliefs. The book is interesting and a valuable lesson in how diverse the homeschooling world has become.

*Cohen, Cafi. *Homeschoolers' College Admissions Handbook: Preparing 12- to 18-Year-Olds for Success in the College of Their Choice.* Roseville, CA: Prima, 2000.

This book gives specific information about the various ways homeschoolers can prepare themselves for the college admissions process. Cohen demystifies her topic through straightforward, practical advice and addresses a variety of homeschooling styles and philosophies. This book covers much the same material as Cohen's *And What about College? How Homeschooling Leads to Admissions to the Best Colleges and Universities* (Holt Associates, 2000), but *Homeschoolers' College Admissions Handbook* is more recent and has a more user-friendly format. Larger libraries may want to consider investing in both titles.

*Cohen, Cafi. *Homeschooling the Teen Years: Your Complete Guide to Successfully Homeschooling the 13- to 18-Year-Old.* New York: Three Rivers Press, 2000.

Like other books in this series, this one provides a useful guide for more eclectic homeschoolers who are working with teens on building advanced skills and preparing for college and a career. It includes many references to other resources, including curriculums and learning materials, on each subject.

*Dobson, Linda. *Homeschooling the Early Years: Your Complete Guide to Successfully Homeschooling the 3- to 8-Year-Old Child.* New York: Three Rivers Press, 1999.

More eclectic homeschoolers will welcome this book, which explains how children acquire basic skills and concepts and offers suggestions for ways parents can work with children to build these skills. It includes many references to other resources, including curriculums and learning materials, on each subject.

*Dobson, Linda. *The Ultimate Book of Homeschooling Ideas: 500+ Fun and Creative Learning Activities for Kids Ages 3–12.* New York: Three Rivers Press, 2002.

Dobson offers a compendium of activities and ideas she compiled from homeschoolers worldwide. Chapters center on particular subject areas, including chapters on group activities, life skills, and organization; also included are booklists and numerous references to books and other sources of information. The library is mentioned frequently, and there are even a few activities geared toward learning how to use the library more effectively. This practical and excellent resource will be useful to a wide range of homeschoolers.

*Duffy, Cathy. *100 Top Picks for Homeschool Curriculum: Choosing the Right Curriculum and Approach for Your Child's Learning Style.* Nashville, TN: Broadman and Holman, 2005.

Far from a simple listing of her favorite curriculum packages, active homeschooler, lecturer, and writer Cathy Duffy introduces readers to various movements and trends in homeschooling, helps parents formulate their own educational philosophies and goals, and discusses the idea of learning styles. This book is a boon for families trying to navigate the ever-growing world of curriculum options and is an excellent choice for librarians who want to learn more about the materials some families use to homeschool. Duffy writes from a Christian perspective but also includes open-minded reviews of secular curriculum options. Additional reviews and resources can be found on Duffy's website (http://www.cathyduffyreviews.com).

*Gardner, Howard. *Frames of Mind: The Theory of Multiple Intelligences.* New York: Basic Books, 2004.

Gardner is the creator of the theory of multiple intelligences, and his book-length treatment of the subject is an educational milestone. This somewhat dense tome is not for every reader (who may prefer

Thomas Armstrong's more reader-friendly treatment of the subject), but it is an important book for most collections.

*Henry, Shari. *Homeschooling the Middle Years: Your Complete Guide to Successfully Homeschooling the 8- to 12-Year-Old Child*. Roseville, CA: Prima, 1999.

Like other books in this series, this one provides a useful guide for more eclectic homeschoolers beginning to work with children to build more advanced academic skills. It includes many references to other resources, including curriculums and learning materials, on each subject.

*Hirsch, E. D., Jr. *Core Knowledge Series*. New York: Doubleday, 1997–2006.

This series, currently in its second revision, begins with *What Your Kindergartner Needs to Know: Preparing Your Child for a Lifetime of Learning* and works its way year-by-year to *What Your Sixth Grader Needs to Know: Fundamentals of a Good Sixth-Grade Education*. This series is of interest to educators and parents of children in institutional schools as much as it is to homeschooling parents. It provides content and skills benchmarks for each grade and suggests resources for further information and developing skills. Homeschoolers seeking to design their own curriculums, evaluate existing packaged curriculums, or evaluate their children's academic progress will find these particularly useful.

*Llewellyn, Grace. *The Teenage Liberation Handbook: How to Quit School and Get a Real Life and Education*. Eugene, OR: Lowry House, 1998.

This book geared toward teenagers (but equally useful to parents) explores how teens can get a high-quality education by being involved in real work and doing what they love outside of institutional schools. Llewellyn's approach is light and readable, and her guidance is solid for homeschoolers who are comfortable with less structure.

*Penn-Nabrit, Paula. *Morning by Morning: How We Home-Schooled Our African-American Sons to the Ivy League*. New York: Villard, 2003.

Penn-Nabrit's story of how she and her husband chose to remove their sons from preparatory school and educate them at home is a story about family, faith, the value of education, and overcoming obstacles. The author's candid approach is funny, inspiring, and thought provoking and is a worthwhile read even for those who have little interest in homeschooling.

Princiotta, Daniel, and Stacey Bielick. *Homeschooling in the United States: 2003.* Washington, DC: National Center for Education Statistics, 2005.

This report contains the most comprehensive and nonbiased statistical information currently available on homeschoolers. It explores demographics, reasons for homeschooling, and sources of learning materials. The Center plans to conduct a follow-up study in 2007. For more information, visit http://nces.ed.gov/pubs2006/homeschool/.

Stevens, Mitchell L. *Kingdom of Children: Culture and Controversy in the Homeschooling Movement.* Princeton, NJ: Princeton University Press, 2001.

This book-length sociological study of the development of the homeschooling movement in the Chicago area provides fascinating insights into how the homeschooling movement is organized, why homeschooling has been able to flourish in the United States, and where stereotypes about homeschoolers come from.

*Trelease, Jim. *The Read-Aloud Handbook.* 6th ed. New York: Penguin Books, 2006.

Although not written expressly for homeschoolers, Trelease's book contains a wealth of useful information about how to develop reading skills as well as a love of reading and high-quality literature. It also provides excellent read-aloud suggestions.

Homeschooling Philosophies

*Bauer, Susan Wise, and Jessie Wise. *The Well-Trained Mind: A Guide to Classical Education at Home.* New York: W. W. Norton, 2004.

This hefty book is the standard for homeschoolers who follow the classical model. Bauer and Wise provide the philosophy behind classical homeschooling, detailed information about implementing a classical homeschooling plan for kindergarten through the twelfth grade, and information about practical matters such as scheduling and dealing with standardized tests.

*Cooper, Elaine, ed. *When Children Love to Learn: A Practical Application of Charlotte Mason's Philosophy for Today.* Wheaton, IL: Crossway Books, 2004.

> This introduction to Mason's educational philosophies also provides practical advice for parents who want to apply Mason's approach to their homeschooling.

*Gatto, John Taylor. *Dumbing Us Down: The Hidden Curriculum of Compulsory Schooling.* Gabriola Island, BC, Canada: New Society Publishers, 2005.

> Award-winning former public school teacher Gatto's treatise on the U.S. economy's dependence on schools that teach such values as conformity and a dependence on other people's ideas and opinions argues that institutional schools can never provide what he considers a true education. Gatto's ideas have influenced many homeschoolers.

*Griffith, Mary. *The Unschooling Handbook: How to Use the Whole World as Your Child's Classroom.* Rocklin, CA: Prima, 1998.

> This book provides a clear, concise, unintimidating introduction to unschooling. Griffith uses exposition, studies, and anecdotes from real homeschoolers to show how unschooling works. She makes unschooling sound both appealing and possible, covering everything from how children learn to how families can make unschooling economically feasible. Each chapter ends with resource lists that include books, websites, catalogs, and other relevant resources.

*Guterson, David. *Family Matters: Why Homeschooling Makes Sense.* New York: Harcourt Brace Jovanovich, 1992.

> This book is somewhat dated and occasionally awkward, but Guterson's considered perspective as an open-minded homeschooler and public school teacher is interesting and thought provoking. One of the most carefully considered works on the philosophy behind homeschooling and what education means in our society.

*Holt, John. *How Children Fail.* Reading, MA: Addison-Wesley, 1995; and *How Children Learn.* Reading, MA: Addison-Wesley, 1995.

> These books were both originally published in 1964 and, combined, provide the philosophy behind unschooling. *How Children Fail* focuses on what Holt saw in classrooms as a teacher, assistant, and observer. In *How Children Learn,* Holt explores how very young

children effectively use games, experiments, fantasy, and good-old hard work to learn about things that interest them.

*Kohn, Alfie. *Punished by Rewards: The Trouble with Gold Stars, Incentive Plans, A's, Praise, and Other Bribes.* Boston: Houghton Mifflin, 1999.

Kohn's exploration of the dangers of extrinsic motivation and how one can go about building intrinsic motivation is already a staple in many libraries. Although this book is not about homeschooling, Kohn's ideas have influenced many homeschoolers.

*Moore, Raymond, and Dorothy Moore. *The Successful Homeschool Family Handbook: A Creative and Stress-Free Approach to Homeschooling.* Nashville, TN: Thomas Nelson, 1994.

The Moores played an important role in popularizing homeschooling, especially among conservative Protestants, in the 1970s and '80s. This admittedly dense book covers most of the philosophies and ideas the Moores developed in their other writings, including the "Moore Formula," which encourages parents to teach children through study, manual labor, and service. Although the Moores' ideas are not in vogue today, the book gives an important bit of history and a different perspective on how conservative Protestants might approach homeschooling.

Faith-Based Homeschooling

*Madden, Kristin. *Pagan Homeschooling: A Guide to Adding Spirituality to Your Child's Education.* Niceville, FL: Spilled Candy Books, 2002.

This book provides a basic introduction to homeschooling as well as suggestions and ideas for ways to incorporate spirituality into every aspect of the homeschooling experience.

*Pride, Mary. *Mary Prides's Complete Guide to Getting Started in Homeschooling.* Eugene, OR: Harvest House, 2004.

This book evolved from Pride's several editions of *The Big Book of Home Learning*, the first book to review homeschooling curriculums. This book continues the tradition of recommending and reviewing resources with a conservative Protestant filter and also offering information on learning styles, homeschooling methods, and various practical matters.

*Wittmann, Maureen, and Rachel Mackson, eds. *The Catholic Homeschool Companion*. Manchester, NH: Sophia Institute Press, 2005.

This collection of essays by forty-three homeschoolers covers topics such as core subjects, homeschooling styles, homeschooling children with special needs, and coping on a day-to-day basis. All of the authors come from a Catholic perspective and some address specifically Catholic concerns, but many of the essays deal with issues common to all homeschoolers and could be of broader interest.

Homeschooling Children with Special Needs

*Field, Christine M. *Homeschooling the Challenging Child: A Practical Guide*. Nashville, TN: Broadman & Holman, 2005.

Field writes about homeschooling children who have attention and learning disabilities from a Christian perspective that is honest, positive, and could prove useful to people who don't share Field's strong religious beliefs. She addresses practicalities with an emphasis on the spiritual and emotional issues the whole family deals with when a child has particularly challenging learning needs. Field also maintains a website (www.homefieldadvantage.org).

*Hayes, Lenore Colacion. *Homeschooling the Child with ADD (or Other Special Needs): Your Complete Guide to Successfully Homeschooling the Child with Learning Differences*. Roseville, CA: Prima, 2002.

This excellent introduction to homeschooling children with special needs covers federal education law, working with school districts, finding support, and figuring out the nuts and bolts of setting up a curriculum and teaching. Resource lists point parents to a wealth of further information.

*Rivero, Lisa. *Creative Home Schooling: A Resource Guide for Smart Families*. Scottsdale, AZ: Great Potential Press, 2002.

This book focuses on homeschooling children who are gifted, but there is much here that would be helpful to anyone homeschooling an unusual or precocious child. Rivero covers the common characteristics of gifted learners, learning styles, methods of instruction, and different styles of homeschooling. She includes the perspectives, advice, and stories of many homeschoolers—parents and children alike. Her resource lists are tremendously useful for the parents of gifted children and the librarians who serve them.

Professional Resources: Collection Development

Baker, Sharon L., and Karen L. Wallace. *The Responsive Public Library: How to Develop and Market a Winning Collection.* 2nd ed. Englewood, CO: Libraries Unlimited, 2002.

This book provides an exhaustive guide to developing and marketing a collection based on input from library users. Baker and Wallace's enthusiastic approach and attention to concepts such as marketing segmentation offer a great deal of useful information to librarians building homeschooling collections.

Biblarz, Dora, Stephen Bosch, and Chris Sugnet, eds. *Guide to Library User Needs Assessment for Integrated Information Resource Management and Collection Development.* Lanham, MD: Scarecrow Press, 2001.

This concise guide, compiled under the name of the Association for Library Collections and Technical Services (a division of the American Library Association), gives the basics of performing a needs assessment with an eye toward collection development.

Johnson, Peggy. *Fundamentals of Collection Development and Management.* Chicago: American Library Association, 2004.

Johnson leads librarians through every step of developing a collection, from planning to promotion. The book provides a nice balance between philosophical concerns and practical advice.

Walker, Barbara J. *The Librarian's Guide to Developing Christian Fiction Collections for Children.* New York: Neal-Schuman, 2005; and *The Librarian's Guide to Developing Christian Fiction Collections for Young Adults.* New York: Neal-Schuman, 2005.

Libraries with a large Christian homeschooling population should consider beefing up their Christian fiction collections. These excellent guides give librarians a solid introduction to the world of Christian publishing and provide core lists to help build collections.

Professional Resources: Program Development

American Association of School Librarians and Association for Educational Communications and Technology. *Information Power: Building Partnerships for Learning.* Chicago: American Library Association, 1998.

> Created through a partnership between the AASL and AECT, this book provides a listing of information literacy standards along with indicators, levels of proficiency, and examples for each standard. This standard text influences the programs developed by school library media specialists in schools all over the United States.

Driggers, Preston, and Eileen Dumas. *Managing Library Volunteers: A Practical Toolkit.* Chicago: American Library Association, 2002.

> This book focuses on the basics of building volunteer programs, including a wealth of practical advice, reproducible forms, and samples. It is an excellent introduction to the subject for libraries that want to start a volunteer program or expand an existing program.

Garner, Carolyn. *Teaching Library Media Skills in Grades K–6: A How-to-Do-It Manual for Librarians.* New York: Neal-Schuman, 2004.

> This resource provides information about designing and implementing library skills programs for elementary-age children and includes lesson plans, handouts, and worksheets.

Goldstone, Lawrence, and Nancy Goldstone. *Deconstructing Penguins: Parents, Kids, and the Bond of Reading.* New York: Ballantine Books, 2005.

> The Goldstones explore the benefits of running a parent-child book group with an emphasis on literary criticism. They draw from their years of running successful groups to create a guide that is equal parts theory and practical, nuts-and-bolts advice.

Karp, Rashelle S., ed. *Powerful Public Relations: A How-To Guide for Libraries.* Chicago: American Library Association, 2002.

> This concise resource focuses on the basics of public relations and marketing, including how to create press releases, publications, and public service announcements.

Knowles, Elizabeth, and Martha Smith. *Talk about Books! A Guide for Book Clubs, Literature Circles, and Discussion Groups, Grades 4–8.* Westport, CT: Libraries Unlimited, 2003.

Knowles and Smith provide guides to help librarians plan book discussions for fifteen different books. Each chapter includes a summary of the book, information about the author, discussion questions, a list of related titles, suggestions for ways to tie the book into subject areas, and sources of further information.

Kunzel, Bonnie, and Constance Hardesty. *The Teen-Centered Book Club: Readers into Leaders*. Westport, CT: Libraries Unlimited, 2006.

This guide for running a teen book group provides sound advice as well as examples of successful and innovative programs for teens.

Pfeil, Angela B. *Going Places with Youth Outreach: Smart Marketing Strategies for Your Library*. Chicago: American Library Association, 2005.

Successfully serving homeschoolers is almost certainly going to involve outreach, and Pfeil's thought-provoking guide gives a wide range of information and ideas, for both those new to outreach and those with more experience.

Reid, Rob. *Family Storytime: Twenty-four Creative Programs for All Ages*. Chicago: American Library Association, 1999.

Reid's storytime ideas are perfect for the wide age range one often sees at programs for homeschoolers.

Reid, Rob. *Something Funny Happened at the Library: How to Create Humorous Programs for Children and Young Adults*. Chicago: American Library Association, 2003.

This book offers ideas for storytimes, book parties, reader's theater, and other humorous library programs.

Veldof, Jerilyn. *Creating the One-Shot Library Workshop: A Step-by-Step Guide*. Chicago: American Library Association, 2006.

This results-focused guide provides a wealth of information on creating, running, and evaluating library instruction sessions, particularly ones geared toward teens and parents.

Webber, Desiree, and Sandy Shropshire. *The Kids' Book Club: Lively Reading and Activities for Grades 1–3*. Englewood, CO: Libraries Unlimited, 2001.

Webber and Shropshire discuss the basics of planning and running a book group that focuses on picture books and then offer program plans for fifteen different picture books.

Professional Resources: Teen Services

Gillespie, Kellie M. *Teen Volunteer Services in Libraries.* Lanham, MD: VOYA Books, 2004.

> Gillespie provides a framework for any library seeking to create a teen volunteer program that benefits the library and is a valuable and needed service to teenagers. She includes step-by-step instructions, real-life examples, and a wealth of sample materials useful to those just starting as well as those trying to expand or improve an existing program.

Lerch, Maureen T., and Janet Welch. *Serving Homeschooled Teens and Their Parents.* Westport, CT: Libraries Unlimited, 2004.

> Amid a wealth of other useful information, Lerch and Welch devote a chapter of their book to diverse and creative programming ideas for homeschooled teens.

Tuccillo, Diane P. *Library Teen Advisory Groups.* Lanham, MD: VOYA Books, 2005.

> This comprehensive source contains everything a library needs to start a teen advisory group. Tuccillo begins by explaining the value to libraries of teen advisory groups and then moves into funding issues, getting the group started, and working with the group. She includes concrete examples, model programs, suggestions for further reading, and sample forms and publicity materials.

PERIODICALS

The following lists the major homeschooling magazines active today. Of course, it is the nature of periodicals to start up and go out of print with some regularity, and homeschooling periodicals are even more notorious for this. I have tried to include periodicals that promise to stay active for some time to come.

Heart and Mind: A Resource for Catholic Homeschoolers (ISSN n/a)
P.O. Box 420881
San Diego, CA 92142
http://www.heart-and-mind.com
4 issues/year

> Aimed at Catholic homeschoolers, articles in this quarterly focus on topics such as unit studies, literature, classical homeschooling, practical information, and product reviews.

Home Education Magazine (ISSN: 0888-4633)
P.O. Box 1083
Tonasket, WA 98855-1083
tel: 800-236-3278, or 509-486-1351
http://www.homeedmag.com
6 issues/year

> Often referred to as *HEM*, this magazine takes a secular approach that is unschooler friendly but still useful to other homeschooling approaches. Articles cover a wide range of topics including stories from homeschoolers' daily lives, analysis of news of interest to homeschoolers, and articles on teaching and learning. Potentially useful learning resources are suggested throughout.

Home School Digest (ISSN n/a)
Wisdom's Gate
P.O. Box 374
Covert, MI 49043- 0374
tel: 269-764-1910
http://www.homeschooldigest.com
4 issues/year

> This quarterly journal focuses on matters of philosophy and faith as they apply to conservative Protestant homeschoolers.

Homeschooling Today (ISSN: 1073-2217)
Nehemiah Four, LLC.
P.O. Box 244
Abingdon, VA 24212- 0244
tel: 276-628-7730
http://www.homeschoolingtoday.com
6 issues/year

This conservative Protestant magazine takes a somewhat theme-based approach, mixing philosophical and more practical articles on a topic such as organization or geography. The selection is rounded off with regular columns and product recommendations and reviews.

Life Learning Magazine (ISSN: 1499-7533)
c/o Life Media
P.O. Box 112
Niagara Falls, NY 14304-0112
tel: 1-800-215-9574
http://www.lifelearningmagazine.com
6 issues/year

> This magazine focuses on unschooling, with articles on the learning opportunities and challenges that are part of everyday life.

The Old Schoolhouse Magazine (ISSN n/a)
P.O. Box 8426
Gray, TN 37615
tel: 1-888-718-HOME
http://www.thehomeschoolmagazine.com
4 issues/year

> This hefty quarterly looks at homeschooling from a conservative Protestant perspective. Articles address teaching a variety of subjects to children and teens as well articles of general interest and product reviews.

Practical Homeschooling (ISSN: 1075-4741)
Home Life, Inc.
P.O. Box 1190
Fenton, MO 63026-1190
tel: 636-529-0137, fax: 636-225-0743
http://www.home-school.com
6 issues/year, bimonthly

> Published by prominent homeschooling advocate Mary Pride, this magazine takes a conservative Protestant perspective on the nuts and bolts of homeschooling, including regular columns on topics such as reading, history, math, science, and preparing for college. Each issue includes homeschooling news as well as product announcements and reviews.

INDEX

A
A Beka Book, 24, 91
A Beka Home School Catalog, 87
About.com Homeschooling website, 3
Advanced Training Institute International, 24
advocacy, homeschooling and, 68–69
African American homeschoolers, 46–49
Alice, I Think (Juby), 80
Alpha Omega Publications, 24, 87, 91
And What about College? (Cohen), 16
Andersen, Deborah Lines, 62, 97
Andreola, Karen, 43
Ardantane's School of Shamanic Studies, 31
art materials as resources, 14
artists as homeschoolers, 50
Asperger's syndrome, 37

B
Bahai Homeschooling discussion list, 32
Barnier, Carol, 23–24
Bauer, Susan Wise, 44
Beautiful Feet Books Catalog, 87
Bethel Park Public Library (Pennsylvania), 79
Better Late Than Early (Moore), 21
Big Book of Home Learning (Pride), 23
BJU Press Total Homeschool Solutions, 87
Bob Jones University Press, 24
Book Links, 85
books
    about youth with special needs, 35
    on Charlotte Mason homeschooling, 43–44
    faith-based homeschooling, 125–126
    featuring homeschooling, 80
    general homeschooling resources, 119–123
    homeschooling philosophies, 123–125
    in special collection, 86
    on unschooling movement, 16–17
    on youth with special needs, 126–127
Buddhist homeschoolers, 30, 32

C
California, 9
Calvert School Education Services Catalog, 87
Catholic Family Expo, 27
Catholic Heritage Curricula, 29, 87
The Catholic Home, 27
The Catholic Homeschool Companion (Mackson and Wittman), 28
A Catholic Homeschool Treasury (Mackson and Wittman), 28
Catholic homeschoolers, 2, 26–29, 64
CatholicMom.com, 28
A Charlotte Mason Companion (Andreola), 43
A Charlotte Mason Education (Levinson), 43–44
Charlotte Mason homeschooling, 27, 43–44, 115
Chili Public Library, 113
Chinaberry Catalog, 37, 87
Christian Liberty Press, 87
Christianity. *See* Charlotte Mason homeschooling; *specific religions*
churches, identifying homeschoolers via, 58
classical homeschooling, 44, 115
Clonlara School, 16
Cobblestone, 85
Cohen, Cafi, 16
community, homeschoolers in. *See* homeschoolers in community
conferences, 60
Cooper, Elaine, 44

correspondence programs, 16
Creative Homeschooling (Rivero), 35
Cuisenaire rods, 14, 115
curriculum
    catalog resources, 87
    for Catholic homeschoolers, 29
    defined, 115
    homeschooling options, 6
    for Protestant homeschoolers, 24–25
    unschooling movement and, 15–16
curriculum and supply catalogs, 86–88
curriculum fairs, 60, 115
curriculum kits, 89–90
curriculum swaps, 80

D

DeFore, Jessica, 45
Department of Defense Education Activity (DoDEA), 51
developmental disabilities. *See* youth with special needs
Dewey Decimal System, 71–72, 74–75
Diagnostic Statistical Manual, 37
Dig, 85
diplomas, unschooling movement and, 15–16
discussion lists
    librarians subscribing to, 64
    for military homeschoolers, 51
    for religious homeschoolers, 32
    for unschooling movement, 15
    for youth with special needs, 36
Dobson, James, 21–22
DoDEA (Department of Defense Education Activity), 51
Duffy, Cathy, 22, 35, 45, 86
Dumbing Us Down (Gatto), 17

E

eclectic homeschooling
    Catholics and, 27
    Charlotte Mason homeschooling and, 43
    giftedness and, 39
    overview, 50, 115
    Pagans and, 31
    youth with special needs and, 35

Edmonds Homeschool Resource Center, 9
Educators Publishing Service, 87
Edwards, Fay, 73
environmental concerns, 5
Exceptional Parent Magazine, 85

F

Family Matters (Guterson), 9
Field, Christine M., 35
focus groups, 60–66
Focus on the Family radio show, 21
For the Children's Sake (Macaulay), 43
For the Love of Literature (Wittman), 28
4-H clubs, 58
FUN Books, 12

G

Gantos, Jack, 80
Gardner, Howard, 37, 116
Garner, Carolyn, 73–75
Gatto, John Taylor, 17
GED program, 16
Generation Joshua, 23
giftedness, 39, 115. *See also* youth with special needs
Gillespie, Kellie M., 66
Goddess Moon Circles Academy, 30
Griffith, Mary, 17–18
Growing without Schooling (GWS), 12
Guilderland Public Library, 97
Guterson, David, 9
GWS (*Growing without Schooling*), 12

H

Hahn, Lynn, 79
Hannigan, Katherine, 80
Hayes, Lenore Colacion, 37–38
Heart and Mind, 27–28
Henderson, Cathy, 71, 74–75
higher education
    homeschooled children and, 7–8
    library programs about, 81
    unschooling movement and, 15–16
high/low books, 115
Hindu homeschoolers, 30
Holt Associates, 12, 115

Holt, John
  formation of Holt Associates, 12, 115
  unschooling philosophy, 2, 4, 11–13, 115
  on volunteering, 65
home charter schools, 9
Home School Digest, 24
Home School Foundation, 23
Home School Legal Defense Association. *See* HSLDA (Home School Legal Defense Association)
Homeschool Diner website, 3
Homeschool World website, 23
Homeschoolers' College Admissions Handbook (Cohen), 16
homeschoolers in community
  advocacy for, 68–69
  conferences, 60
  curriculum fairs, 60
  focus groups, 60–63
  identifying, 55–60
  marketing to, 58, 65
  surveys, 60–63
  on teen advisory boards, 66–68
  as volunteers, 65–66
homeschooling
  African American, 46–48
  by artists, 50
  building special collection for, 82–92
  Charlotte Mason, 27, 43–44, 115
  child welfare and, 6–7
  classical, 44, 115
  curriculum options, 6
  daily schedules, 5–6
  family composition, 4–6
  fiction featuring, 80
  future of, 7–9
  history of, 1–2
  legal issues, 2–4
  library usage, 9–10
  military, 48–51
  Montessori, 44–46
  for religious reasons, 4–5
  resources about, 3, 16–17
  unschooling and, 11
  youth with special needs, 33–41

  See also eclectic homeschooling; religious reasons for homeschooling
The Homeschooling Handbook (Griffith), 17–18
Homeschooling the Challenging Child (Field), 35
Homeschooling the Child with ADD (or Other Special Needs) (Hayes), 38
Homeschooling Today, 24
How Children Fail (Holt), 2, 11
How Children Learn (Holt), 2, 11
How to Get Your Child Off the Refrigerator and On to Learning (Barnier), 23
HSLDA (Home School Legal Defense Association)
  information on state laws, 4, 23
  listings of homeschooling organizations, 57
  military homeschoolers and, 52
  overview, 22–23, 115
  website, 51
HUUMans website, 32, 57

I

Ida B . . . (Hannigan), 80
IEP (Individualized Education Plan), 35
If I'm Diapering a Watermelon, Then Where'd I Leave the Baby? (Barnier), 23
Individualized Education Plan (IEP), 35
Information Power, 73
Internet searches, 57

J

Jefferson, Thomas, 2
Jehovah's Witness homeschoolers, 30, 32
Jewish homeschoolers, 30
JLAMS, 62, 97
job description, project coordinator, 111–112
Johnsburg Public Library (Illinois), 88, 90–92
Journal of College Admission, 7
Juby, Susan, 80

K

Kingdom of Children (Stevens), 7, 20
Kiplinger's Personal Finance Magazine, 50
Klassen, Sue, 59–60
Knapp, Julie Shephard, 3
Kohn, Alfie, 16–17, 86
Kolbe Academy, 29
KONOS, 24

L

Lakeshore Learning Materials, 87
Langford, Janet, 73
language arts instruction, 78–79
LEAH (Loving Education at Home), 64, 101
learning disabilities. *See* youth with special needs
Lee, Carol K., 73
legal issues
   in homeschooling, 2–4
   information on state laws, 4, 23, 42, 51
   for youth with special needs, 36–38
Levinson, Catherine, 43–44
libraries
   Charlotte Mason homeschoolers and, 44
   classical homeschoolers and, 44
   connecting with homeschoolers, 60
   conservative Protestant homeschoolers and, 25
   helping homeschoolers, 93–98
   homeschooling and, 9–10
   identifying homeschoolers, 56–58
   military homeschoolers and, 52–53
   surveys and focus groups, 60–66
   unschooling movement and, 17–19
   volunteering at, 66–68
   youth with special needs and, 38–41
library programs
   age level considerations, 71–72
   basic library skills, 70, 72–75
   curriculum swaps, 80
   displays, 80
   finding fiction by subject, 76–77
   games for library instruction, 73
   for homeschoolers, 77–81
   literacy skills, 73–75
   literature-based, 78–79
   open houses, 78
   orientation, 72
   for parents, 75–77
   preparing for college, 81
   professional resources, 128–130
lifelong learning, 76
Lincoln, Abraham, 2
literacy skills, teaching, 73–75
LivingMathForum discussion list, 15
Llewellyn, Grace, 17
local organizations, 56–58
Loving Education at Home (LEAH), 64, 101
Loyola Press, 87

M

Macaulay, Susan Schaeffer, 43
Mackson, Rachel, 28
Madden, Kristin, 30–31
magazines. *See* periodicals
Magic Dragon, 85
manipulatives, 115
marketing methods, 58, 65
Mason, Charlotte, 43–44, 115
mathematical concepts
   Cuisenaire rods, 14, 115
   for youth with special needs, 37
McCarthy, Amy, 62, 93–95, 97–98
mental health issues. *See* youth with special needs
Merkh, Jonathan, 25
Meyer, Renae, 52–53
military homeschoolers, 48–51
Miller, Pat, 73
Miss America Pageant, 6
mission statements, 113
Monroe County Library System (New York), 95–96
Montessori, Maria, 44–46
Montessori homeschoolers, 44–46
Moon, Valerie Bonham, 49
Moore, Dorothy, 21–22, 65, 115
Moore, Raymond, 21–22, 65, 115
Moore Formula, 21, 115–116
Mormon homeschoolers, 30

Morning by Morning (Penn-Nabrit), 46, 48
Mother of Divine Grace School, 29
multidisciplinary, 116
multimedia, 116
multiple intelligences theory, 37, 116
Muse, 85
musical instruments as resources, 14
Muslim homeschoolers, 30, 32
My Father's World, 87

N

NACHE (National Association of Catholic Homes and Educators), 27
National Association of Catholic Homes and Educators (NACHE), 27
National Center for Education Statistics, 1, 5, 20, 46
National Geographic Bee, 6
National Home Education Network (NHEN), 51
National Home Education Research Institute (NHERI), 3, 116
National Library Service for the Blind and Physically Handicapped, 40–41
New York
 library programs, 71–72, 74–75
 "Serving Homeschoolers" Grant, 95–96, 99–114
NHEN (National Home Education Network), 51
NHERI (National Home Education Research Institute), 3, 116
No Question Left Behind (Wittman), 28

O

The Old Schoolhouse, 24
100 Top Picks for Homeschool Curriculum (Duffy), 22, 35, 45, 86
open houses, 78
Our Lady of the Rosary School, 29
Our Lady of Victory, 29

P

Pagan homeschoolers, 30–31
Pagan Homeschooling (Madden), 30–31
Painton, Melissa, 64–65
Pareto principle, 9
Parma Public Library, 113
pathfinder, 116
Patrick Henry College, 23
Penn-Nabrit, Paula, 46–48
Pennsylvania
 homeschooling requirements, 4
 library programs, 72, 79
"people first" language, 39, 116
periodicals
 for conservative Protestants, 24
 major homeschooling, 130–132
 in special collection, 85–86
phonics, 13–14, 116
Practical Homeschooling, 5, 23–24
Pride, Mary, 5, 23
Prima Publishing, 18
project coordinator job description, 111–112
Protestant homeschoolers, 4–5, 20–25, 57
Publisher's Weekly, 25
Punished by Rewards (Kohn), 16–17, 86

Q

Quaker homeschoolers, 30, 32

R

radical unschooling, 15, 116
RAHA (Rochester Area Homeschoolers Association), 59–60, 64, 101
Ray, Brian D., 3
reading materials. *See* books; periodicals
Real Lives (Llewellyn), 17
realia, 116
religious reasons for homeschooling
 by Buddhists, 30, 32
 by Catholics, 2, 26–29
 discussion lists, 32
 electronic discussion lists, 32
 by Hindus, 30
 by Jehovah's Witnesses, 30, 32
 by Jews, 30
 by Mormons, 30
 by Muslims, 30, 32
 by Pagans, 30–31
 by Protestants, 4–5, 20–25
 by Quakers, 30, 32

resources
   on collection development, 127
   fiction featuring homeschooling, 80
   for homeschooling, 3, 16–17
   on program development, 128–130
   for youth with special needs, 35–36
   on teen services, 130
   for unschooling movement, 14–17
   See also books; discussion lists; periodicals; websites
Rivero, Lisa, 35
Rochester Area Homeschoolers Association (RAHA), 59–60, 64, 101
Rosetta Stone, 91

S

safety, homeschooling for, 5
Scholastic Early and Primary Reading Catalog, 87
school-at-home, 116
scientific equipment as resource, 14
scouting organizations, 58
Scripps Howard National Spelling Bee, 6
"Serving Homeschoolers" Grant, 95–96, 99–114
Seton Home Study School, 29
Seventh-Day Adventist religion, 21
Seymour Library, 113
Shluchim Office, 30
Singapore Math, 91
Smith, Catherine Arnott, 39
socialization of homeschoolers, 7, 34–35
Sonlight Curriculum Catalog, 87
special collections
   books in, 86
   creating collection statement, 83–84
   curriculum and supply catalogs in, 86–88
   curriculum kits, 89–90
   equipment for, 88
   gathering information for, 82–83
   housing, 85
   manipulatives for, 88
   periodicals in, 85–86
   professional resources, 127
   teaching aids, 88

standard measurements of achievement, 15–16
Stevens, Mitchell L., 7, 20
support groups, identifying, 56–58
surveys for homeschoolers, 60–66
Surviving the Applewhites (Tolan), 80

T

teaching aids in special collection, 88
Teaching Library Media Skills in Grades K–6 (Garner), 73–75
Teaching Pre K–8, 85
teen advisory boards, 66–68, 116
Teen Ink, 85
teen services, 130
Teen Volunteer Services in Libraries (Gillespie), 66
The Teenage Liberation Handbook (Llewellyn), 17
testing, unschooling movement and, 15–16
Texas, 4
Tolan, Stephanie S., 80
T.O.R.C.H. (Traditions of Roman Catholic Homes), 27
trivium, 116
twice exceptional, 33, 116. *See also* youth with special needs

U

unit studies, 117
Unitarian Universalists, 32, 57
University of Wisconsin–Madison, 39
The Unschooling Handbook (Griffith), 17
unschooling movement
   achievement measurements and, 15–16
   defined, 11–13, 117
   eclectic homeschooling and, 31
   growth of, 2
   libraries connecting with, 17–19
   radical, 15, 116
   resources about, 14–17
   on whole language, 14

V

Viral Learning (Griffith), 18
volunteers, homeschoolers as, 65–66

W

Washington (state), 9
Washington, George, 1
Weaver Curriculum, 24
Webb, Austin, 8
websites
    about Charlotte Mason homeschooling, 43
    about homeschooling, 3
    for African American homeschoolers, 48–49
    for Catholic homeschoolers, 27, 29
    for Jewish homeschoolers, 30
    listings of homeschooling groups, 57
    for military homeschoolers, 49, 51
    for other faiths, 32
    for Pagan homeschoolers, 30
    for Protestant homeschoolers, 23–24

Webster Public Library, 84, 113
Weinert, Marcia, 67–68
The Well-Trained Mind (Bauer and Wise), 44–45
What Would Joey Do? (Gantos), 80
When Children Love to Learn (Cooper), 44
whole language, 13–14, 117
Wise, Jessie, 44
Wittman, Maureen, 28

Y

YMCAs, 58
youth with special needs
    discussion lists, 36
    homeschooling, 33–41
    resources for, 126–127

Z

Zawacki, Maria, 90–92

Adrienne Furness is Children and Family Services Librarian at the Webster Public Library in Webster, New York. She has spent the past decade working with homeschoolers in various settings, providing basic library services as well as targeted programming and collections. She served as administrator of a 2005–2007 NYS Parent and Child Services Grant dedicated to better serving homeschoolers in Monroe County, New York. Adrienne is also a freelance writer whose work has appeared in such publications as *AudioFile Magazine, Book Magazine, St. James Encyclopedia of Popular Culture, Library Journal, School Library Journal,* and *Children and Libraries* and on her blogs at www.watat.com and http://homeschoolingandlibraries.wordpress.com.